Philosophy in the N

C000104500

For Ed Colyer, Patrick Harpur
and Guthrie McGruer (see page 23)

Philosophy in the New Century

Anthony O'Hear

continuum
LONDON • NEW YORK

Continuum

The Tower Building
11 York Road
London SE1 7NX

15 East 26th Street
New York
NY 10010

www.continuumbooks.com

© 2001 Anthony O'Hear

First published 2001
This edition 2003

British Library Cataloguing-in-Publication Data
A catalogue record for this book is available from the British Library.

ISBN   0-8264-7132-3

Typeset by Kenneth Burnley, Wirral, Cheshire.
Printed and bound in Great Britain by MPG Books Ltd, Bodmin, Cornwall

Contents

Introduction

The twentieth century saw great hopes but also great failures. Alongside technological triumphs and unprecedented scientific advances, there have been ecological disasters and, among many, a fear of science. There have been great political projects and hopes and, at the same time, political regimes of unparalleled evil. There were two world wars, alongside a steady increase in wealth and population throughout the world. And while, in the second half of the century, much of the world has come to take peace and democracy for granted, tyranny, war and oppression remain the norm for many.

In those parts of the world characterized by increasing prosperity and by liberal democracy, there has at the same time been an erosion of traditional beliefs and values. For example, religious faith declined precipitately, and with it many practices and customs formerly taken for granted. As in life more generally, a mood of uncertainty and experiment characterized the arts and literature in the twentieth century.

In the upheavals and dilemmas presented by the twentieth century, what did philosophy have to offer? Did it provide a rudder, enabling people to steer their way through the troubling and often conflicting waters of the times, or did it swim with whatever currents it found itself in?

Cultural historians would see philosophy, as other subjects and disciplines, as reflecting the times which produce it. But philosophy, surely, claims to be getting at timeless truths, truths which might confront and embarrass fashion, and which might, in their difficulties, give people pointers by which to steer.

Unfortunately, as I suggest in the opening chapter of this book, twentieth-century philosophy did not have an impressive record when dealing with twentieth-century fashion. Too often, in its leading exemplars, it simply went along with fashions, in particular with scientific fashions and with political fashions. In typical twentieth-century manner, much twentieth-century philosophy tried to be radical and to find a fresh new start away from what its proponents took to be the dross of the past. But in striving for a new start, it swept away too much of value, too much of what was needed to keep one's humanity intact.

One leading school of twentieth-century philosophy tended to look to science as the model of inquiry and the touchstone of truth, while the other has been engaged on a relentless critique of normality in a search for the grail of authenticity. In doing so, both schools, as I will argue, ran up against dead ends. And, whether this is cause or effect, in both schools it is hard to find writing which is not clogged with jargon and technicality, of relevance to few who are not involved with philosophy professionally. In saying these things, the point is not to blame those who set out on these journeys, from whom we can learn much, and in whose work there is much to wonder at. The point is to learn from what has happened.

So the question to which this book is primarily addressed is where, in the new century, philosophy ought to go. In giving my answer, I am far from dismissing the work of philosophers of the twentieth century. So there is a second question, which I hope to some extent to answer. Is it possible to re-configure the current philosophical landscape in such a way as to keep faith with those who look to philosophy to throw light on fundamental questions of life and how it should be lived? For it is these questions which draw most people to philosophy in the first place, only then to discover professional philosophers making huge efforts to avoid them.

If philosophy is to have a future in the twenty-first century, it must not sacrifice rigour. But to regain relevance and significance, it must turn away from scientism and cultural nihilism, the philosophical dead-ends of the twentieth century.

1 Wisdom

Philosophy means love of wisdom. So, in thinking philo-sophically, can we expect to gain wisdom? Will philosophy help us to live better? Should it? Or is philosophy just an academic study, interesting in itself, but with no particular bearing on the rest of life?

It is certainly true that philosophy is not the same as religion, and never has been. Philosophy does not pretend to bring us revelations about the ultimate purpose of the universe or the intentions of its creator, if there is one. Philosophy, even that of a profoundly religious thinker like St Thomas Aquinas, stays self-consciously within the limits of what human reason can discover about things.

Its wisdom, such as it is, is what can be gleaned by reflection on the world and human experience without the benefit of teachings from sacred scriptures or the revelations of gods or would-be prophets. Aquinas, indeed, clearly separated truths he believed could be shown by reason (philosophy), from those he thought could only be based on divine revelation (theology). Neither does philosophy prescribe rituals or codes of practice for believers.

Further, as anyone with even the smallest knowledge of the history of philosophy will be aware, while some philosophers have thought it possible to show philosophically that God does exist, many others, particularly nowadays, have disagreed. This observation simply prompts the question as to whether, with disagreements on so fundamental a matter as the existence of God, can philosophy – particularly philosophy today – provide us with anything approximating to wisdom? In answering this question, it is necessary to take a broad historical perspective.

Philosophy, as we in the West understand it at the start of the third millennium, has its origins in classical Greece, in the fifth and sixth centuries BC. While we know only a little about their predecessors, we know a considerable amount about the great trio of Socrates, Plato and Aristotle, and also about their successors, the schools of philosophy which flourished in Hellenistic and Roman times. Socrates, Plato and Aristotle were certainly interested in some abstruse and abstract questions, which they discussed in great and meticulous detail. But it is clear that, over and above the detail, each conceived philosophy as a discipline leading to wisdom about the best way to live and about one's place in the universe. And so did their Hellenistic and Roman successors. This agreement about philosophy's ultimate purpose transcended disagreements about such matters as the existence or non-existence of God.

Indeed, to take a striking example, the Epicurean philosophy, immortalized in Lucretius's great poem 'De Rerum Natura', is precisely an attempt to draw out the consequences for living of the materialism and atheism of that school of philosophy.

One could argue that wisdom remained a part, albeit a not always very prominent part, of the ambition of much philosophy until comparatively recently. That is to say, many of those generally considered to be the great philosophers saw their philosophy as part of an attempt to expound a vision of man's place in the universe, and, by extension, a vision of how life should be lived in the light of that vision, whether that vision was compatible with religious belief or not. Often, in either case, the outcome was an expression of something not too distant from wisdom in the traditional sense.

What, though, is also true is that if one is to judge by its most famous and distinguished exponents, philosophy in the twentieth century has seemed far removed from anything which would in the past have been recognizable as wisdom. There is, indeed, a major division within twentieth-century philosophy, between the cool reasoning of the Anglo–American tradition and the hyper-charged jargon and rhetoric of the European. But, whether by default or by intention, both of these traditions undermine 'wisdom' rather than uphold it.

The Anglo–American tradition owes its origin to the work of Bertrand Russell in the first decades of the century. Russell, along with his Cambridge contemporary G. E. Moore, consciously and deliberately attempted to rid philosophy of the obscurity and oracularity with which it had become enmeshed. While nineteenth-century philosophy had not, on the whole, been religiously orthodox, much of it was clearly an attempt to gain the benefits of religious uplift without the cost of implausible dogma, and the means chosen was a mist of obscurity through which rays of inspiration would occasionally break. In the Russell–Moore revolution, clear analysis and pellucid reasoning would replace high-minded windbaggery and pretentious jargon.

These were not ignoble aims, then or now. But to them Russell added the belief that the ideal tool for analysis and reasoning was the formal logical system he himself had been developing along with the German philosopher and mathematician Gottlob Frege. Armed with this method, philosophy would approach the rigour and precision of natural science, which to many twentieth-century philosophers has been the paradigm, if not the only case, of a sound intellectual discipline. Philosophy would itself become a sort of science, both in the way it was conducted and in the decisiveness of its conclusions.

To look at some of the leading philosophical journals of our day, one can see that the first of these ambitions has been amply achieved. The pages of *Mind* or *The Philosophical Review* are bespattered with symbols. The language in which the articles are written is a strange and, to the outsider, largely impenetrable dialect of English, if indeed it is English at all. The themes and questions are so dressed up in technicality as to disguise any human resonance or interest which might lie within them. And these dismal characteristics obtain even when the topic is ostensibly one in the more obviously humane branches of philosophy, such as ethics or aesthetics or political philosophy (which, in any case, are not the areas where the most admired work is being done).

The quasi-scientific way philosophy has been dressed up in the Anglo–American tradition might be justifiable had it achieved results of a stature comparable to those achieved in twentieth-century maths or physics. In fact, precisely the opposite has been the case. From Russell's own attempt to explain mathematics in terms of logic onwards, every major research programme of Anglo–American philosophy in the twentieth century has ended in failure. At least they have ended in failure if failure is a pretty conclusive demonstration of the impossibility of achieving what they set out to demonstrate.

These include attempts to show how all knowledge is based on sense experience (Russell, Ayer), how meaning is based on the so-called verification principle, according to which all meaningful statements are either true by definition or verifiable through sense experience (Ayer), how scientific reasoning can be formalized (Carnap, Popper), how all natural languages are founded on the same underlying grammatical principles (Chomsky), how meaning can be systematically analysed in terms of truth (Davidson), how mental states and events 'supervene' on the physical (Kim), and how morality and politics can be envisaged as the quasi-economic enterprise of working out how as many people's preferences as possible can be simultaneously realized. None of these programmes has been carried through, and it may be no coincidence that most of them involve treating phenomena like natural language and ordinary human experience scientifically or quasi-scientifically.

In fact human reality is simply too multifarious to be constrained in this way, and while that itself may be taken to be a 'result' of twentieth-century analytical philosophy, it is not the one its leading protagonists wanted, except by default. Or, to put it more bluntly, in the words of Nicholas Capaldi, 'think of the abandoned enterprises of Frege, Russell, Carnap, Davidson, Chomsky, etc. It would be difficult to imagine physicists honouring their colleagues for hypotheses that failed to work.'[1] But, in the present philosophical climate, it is doubtful that this will stop the honouring. Neither will this lesson prevent other similar research programmes being instigated which will, like their predecessors, eventually run into the ground.

Not all contemporary philosophy conceives itself as a sort of science. This is certainly not the case with what is often called continental philosophy, that is, philosophy whose leading protagonists in the middle of the century were Heidegger and Sartre, and whose more recent sources of inspiration have been mainly French, writers like Barthes, Foucault, Derrida and Lacan. This style of philosophy rejects the claims of the sciences to give us the basic truth about the physical world, but those who conclude from this that it is likely to have a more humane face than the aridity of the Anglo-Saxon tradition are in for a disappointment.

Its main protagonists have exhibited an apparently inextinguishable penchant for extremist politics. Heidegger was once an enthusiastic Nazi, Sartre an equally unashamed advocate of Stalinism and Maoism, and their successors have been drawn to many different forms of subversive thought and practice. Nor is this pure coincidence. It is not something which can simply be shrugged off as irrelevant to the philosophy. For all these philosophies are ultimately forms of nihilism.

In his early thought Heidegger had advocated a form of authenticity which entailed that the individual tear himself away from the mores of everyday existence, and also from the type of thinking and practice which, according to Heidegger, had dominated the West since the time of Plato. One problem with Heidegger's prescription was that we have no other type of thinking to think with, and no language other than that of the everyday.

This leads directly to a dilemma. If Heideggerian thought is readily intelligible and clearly expressed, it will itself suffer from the very defects Heidegger is trying to avoid. As he himself once put it, 'to make oneself understood is suicidal to philosophy'.[2]

On the other hand, if, as Heidegger did, he constructs a new type of language in which to express this new type of thinking, both language and thought will be closed to all but initiates, who occupy its forms from the inside as it were, fastidiously refraining from corrosive encounters with the world outside.

What beneath the obscurity Heidegger is trying to express is the thought that though there is no God, there is nonetheless some nameless and unspeakable ground of being with whom we human beings stand in a special relationship, which we can develop by living authentically. But what is that? Clearly it cannot be by living 'normally', which, by definition is the inauthentic form of life Heidegger is trying to expose and avoid. What started as a project of lonely and self-dramatizing individualism passes seamlessly into the thought that the only hope for anyone was identification with a deeper reality than that of everyday bourgeois existence. It turned out, in Heidegger's view, to be identification with one's primordial *Volk* and with its leader, he who has burst asunder everyday normality, who 'himself and alone is the present and future German reality and its law'.[3]

Heidegger himself once praised Hitler and Mussolini as being 'the two men who launched counter-movements in Europe'[4] against the nihilism prophesied by Nietzsche and against what Heidegger thought of as the disintegration of human life. But the nihilism and disintegration inveighed against by Heidegger actually amount to just those facets of existence which most people would regard as constituting some of the better aspects of twentieth-century life: liberty, prosperity, democracy, peace, the free market, bourgeois order and settled relationships, and the attempt to sustain these values in the face of Nietzsche's much-heralded, but possibly premature death of God. One may be forgiven for asking just who is the nihilist here.

Sartre shares much of Heidegger's basic philosophical orientation, embellishing it with some brilliant sketches and illustrations. What he adds is an utterly destructive, though not wholly implausible analysis of sexual love. Love cannot be a communion of equals, because the lover wants to possess not just the flesh of the beloved but her freedom and her consciousness too. This, of course, is impossible. Two consciousnesses cannot be one. I cannot possess her consciousness and her freedom, nor she mine. But what can happen is that one consciousness is submerged and suppressed by the other. For Sartre the inevitable frustration of sexual desire leads inexorably to the two extremes of suppression of the other or suppression by the other, sadism or masochism.

More generally, according to Sartre, if I accede to any of the roles which the public world might assign me, I will be sinking my own freedom in the projects and dictates of others. In thus living inauthentically, 'in bad faith' in Sartre's terms, I allow others to steal the world and my freedom from me. In that very precise sense, according to Sartre's own most famous aphorism, 'Hell is other people.'

But, actually and like Heidegger, Sartre does find redemption from the isolation of individual authenticity against inauthentic world in a revolutionary collectivity. Initially in Sartre's case it was as a fellow-traveller of French and Russian communism. When that became too tainted and, in Sartre's view, too right-wing, he threw his weight behind various Maoist groups in France and also behind movements of national liberation outside France, who, in Sartre's view, could achieve a kind of therapeutic purification in acts of terror and violence against the colonialist oppressor.

The suspicion is, as with Heidegger, that it is not others *per se* who are objectionable, but only others who choose to live in conformity with the norms of existing society. The Sartre–Heidegger protest is against the existing norms and structures of Western society, which they see as inherently inauthentic and repressive, and hence as needing to be torn down. That these norms and structures might actually be the condition of the very authenticity and freedom they crave – and indeed of their freedom to think and express their dreams of subversion – entirely escapes them.

As it does Michel Foucault. For Foucault, underlying the forms of conventional twentieth-century existence is a vast, impersonal and invisible network of power relations, which hold us all in check. By means of pedantic and tendentious though often interesting historical analyses, he attempts to convince his readers that notions like crime, punishment, madness, and male and female sexuality are in fact social and historical constructs, with little or no basis in nature, human or otherwise.

Indeed, part of the aim of Foucault's thought can be seen as the denial of any notion of human nature, or at least of any which should be allowed to play any part in ethical or political deliberations. For invoking human nature to justify social orders and structures simply reinforces the dominant power relations which have actually produced in us the prejudice that certain classifications and ways of behaving are 'normal'. Hence, doubtless, the obsession of those influenced by Foucault with science fiction and trans-gressive sexuality, in which normality is systematically unravelled, in the modern jargon 'deconstructed'.

For Jacques Derrida, it is not just human nature which is deconstructed. As far as one can tell from his ever more labyrinthine writings, it is the world itself. Moving swifty (far too swiftly) from the truism that we can only think and speak about anything through our own forms of thought and language, Derrida concludes that we can never escape from what he must regard as the prison of our language and thought. Any attempt to explain what we mean or think only produces yet more streams of language and thought. We can never get out of language into the world itself. Worse, things which are said or thought are subject to multiple interpreta-tion, so their meanings cannot be definitively tied down.

So the world is always interpreted to us through texts. But at root the words which make up these texts are arbitrary: there is no reason why 'table' should mean table, or indeed any precise definition of what it does mean. The abitrariness and uncertainly of words extends even more to the texts they make up. Texts have no definite meaning, but only unending processes of interpretation by yet more texts, over which their producers have no control or authority. So there is no author of these texts responsible for their meaning, and no accessible world, but only more and more texts standing between us and the world whose meaning can never be grasped or tied down with any conviction or certainty.

Out of all this is meant to come the message that, just as world and meaning have disappeared, so has the self. There are only texts uttered by the self, which then elude the grasp of their originator. But 'I', as thought or spoken, am also a text, and so are the things I or others might want to say about me. The real self, the substantial I which might or might not underlie my utterance, cannot be grasped except through the veil of texts, and so it too drops out of contention.

'*Il n'y a pas d'hors texte*', we are asked to concede, leaving it uncertain whether Derrida's strictures about the uncertainty of texts are to be applied to his own texts as well as those of others. No doubt his tediously 'playful' style is meant to convey some kind of self-referential message, but it is doubtful how far we are intended to take this. After all, Derrida appears to be quite serious (though hardly very daring) in his condemnations of racism in France. More to the point, we should ask what the effect of his and Foucault's doctrines are. In the deconstruction of existing reality, language and power structures, what appears to be intended is the liberation of the deconstuctor from all existing constraints. This is partly why those who engage in this sort of process are interested in it, and what they hope to achieve from it. Far from amounting to the denial of the self, deconstruction is the ultimate assertion of self, of the self of the deconstructor. Hell is indeed other people, a hell from which the self stifled by bourgeois convention has to escape by deconstructing everything in the world around him.

I shall argue later that this attempt is, in fact, incoherent. There can be no self apart from others. I have no identity without a social setting in which that identity is initially forged and recognized. A partial recognition of this point may indeed explain why the deconstructors of the everyday, from Heidegger onwards, were all attracted to revolutionary collectivities. Their individualistic nihilism needed and needs a public realm in which to act. But having rejected the actual public realm, which, paradoxically, sustains their dreams of liberation, they are then led to the destructive and hate-fuelled politics of revolutionary fantasy with, all too often, dire results.

There are dire results also for our ordinary conceptions of ourselves, as free agents, as seekers after truth, as beings impelled by considerations of justice, goodness and beauty. Insofar as we remain within the normal understanding of any of these notions, we are, according to the deconstructors, prisoners of our societies. These notions, as ordinarily expounded and understood, are simply reflections of and upholders of the systems of thought and value systems adopted by those in power, by which we are all kept in a state of subservience.

All this is expounded in contemporary 'European' philosophy in a language impenetrable to those not within its charmed circle – and maybe not entirely penetrable even to its initiates. In 1996 the prestigious academic journal *Social Text* published as a serious contribution an article by the physicist Alan Sokal entitled 'Transgressing the Boundaries: Toward a Transformative Hermeneutics of Quantum Gravity'.[5] The article was a deliberate parody of deconstructive doctrines and methods. It was full of confusions and *non-sequiturs*, and also of sheer nonsense. According to Sokal's article (though not, of course, according to Sokal himself), 'physical "reality", no less than social "reality"' is 'at bottom a social and linguistic construct'. Further, that scientific knowledge, far from being objective, 'reflects and encodes the dominant ideologies and power relations of the culture that produced it' with its truth claims being, in consequence, 'inherently theory-laden and self-referential'. Most significant of all, the article was replete with references and quotations from leading post-modernist thinkers espousing versions of the extreme relativism we have seen in examining Derrida and Foucault.

Needless to say, the Sokal hoax has had no tendency to stem the flow of deconstructivist texts: there are too many vested interests at stake. But there is little there for ordinary people, and certainly no wisdom. What they are offered is only a portentous jargon they cannot understand (even if the editors of *Social Text* can), but which nonetheless leaves uninitiated readers with a worrying sense that all their most common-sensical beliefs and cherished ideals need de-masking and de-constructing.

Despite their obvious differences, particularly in their styles and their respective evaluations of the truth and value of science, Anglo–American and continental philosophy converge on a number of points. Both are written in such a way as to exclude the majority of readers. Both deny human freedom, at least on any ordinary understanding of the idea. Both see the individual in materialistic terms, and tend to explain away our pretensions to higher values, as either simply false or a product of false consciousness. Both see no particular difficulty in medical and scientific developments which many would see as highly threatening to human dignity, the one on generally materialistic grounds, the other on the grounds that there is no fixed human nature. Both repudiate any higher wisdom, and hence the ability of philosophy to deliver any wisdom. All we are left with are, on the one hand, scientifically based accounts of human life; or, on the other, deconstruction of the human world.

One might wonder whether, in these circumstances, there was any point in doing philosophy at all. For, although philosophers rarely turn their own critical weapons on their own cherished doctrines, in consistency they should; and if they are not prepared to do so, the rest of us should. Once we do so, both the styles of philosophy we have been examining demonstrate their own impossibility.

In the one case there is nothing to be said which cannot be given in scientific terms, but this doctrine itself is not part of science or required by science. So the doctrine needs a justification framed in terms which it has already by implication declared illegitimate. And in accepting this justification we need to have confidence that we are accepting it freely and rationally, and are not merely being caused to accept it by the workings of material forces in us, over which we have no control. In seeing us as determined by material forces outside our control, materialism removes from us the possibility that what we believe and decide might be rationally decided by us after free inquiry. It thus undermines its own credentials as a doctrine to be accepted on rational grounds, for on its own account people believe things only because physical forces compel them to do so.

In the other case, we are told that our language and thought are fatally contaminated by false consciousness, or are subject to endless and inconclusive interpretation never to reach the world or truth. But we are not given any reason to think that the same things are not true of the philosophies which deliver these doleful messages.

Neither way is there any room for a philosophy or a wisdom which escapes both the restrictions of science and avoids ultimately nihilistic deconstruction and unmasking. But this I believe to be a mistake. I believe that we can reflect on our lives and knowledge and experience in such a way as to avoid either the scientism of the Anglo–Americans or the deconstructive nihilism of the continentals. I believe that we can do this in a way which is both free of jargon and relies only on appeals to experience and rational argument. And I believe that in doing so we can arrive at a conception of ourselves and our world which upholds and articulates many of our traditional and often unthinking beliefs about human dignity. Giving expression to and defence of these traditional beliefs can, without too much distortion, be thought of as a type of wisdom.

In engaging in this task, I will use arguments and appeal to considerations which are the stock-in-trade of modern philosophy. The points I make will be familiar to philosophers, but I hope to deploy them in a constructive way. In particular, I will argue that there are aspects of our experience and existence more fundamental than science, and on which science depends for its possibility. So science cannot be used, as it often is, to undermine those features of our nature. Equally, I will show that the unmasking or deconstructing of the continentals presents us with a picture of ourselves which is a systematic distortion of our experience of ourselves as agents and of the human world; so that picture, too, should be rejected.

But the task is not, of course, primarily negative. It is rather more to suggest that there can be a way forward for philosophy after a period of what from a human perspective has been uncomfortably close to sterility.

2 The Search for Meaning

The great philosopher Socrates was put to death by the state of Athens in 399 BC. His offence was that he had corrupted the youth of Athens and had dishonoured the gods. There was something in these charges. Socrates' personality and, more, his teachings, were disturbing. He did challenge much in conventional wisdom and in the official religion of Athens. But he was in no sense a cynic or a scoffer. He distanced himself from the so-called Sophists, those contemporaries of his who taught the techniques of argument as simply a means of winning legal or political battles and who treated philosophy as a compendium of mind-games. By contrast, in his own relentless philosophical questing and questioning, Socrates was seeking a timeless wisdom, but one which was not dependent on the often disedifying forms and incredible beliefs of established religion.

Socrates himself wrote nothing. Most of what we know of his philosophy comes from the writings of Plato, his devoted pupil and an even greater philosopher. In his Dialogues, Plato expounded and developed Socrates' teaching. Socrates is usually the main character in the Dialogues, although scholars have never ceased to argue about how much there is of the historical Socrates in the various Platonic versions of Socrates (which differ considerably among themselves). But this is a problem which will not concern us here. What I want to do is to consider the account of philosophy which is given in the Dialogue known as *Phaedo.*

In *Phaedo* Plato describes Socrates' last conversation with his friends, as remembered by Phaedo, one of those present. Socrates is in prison waiting to drink the poison which will end his life. During the course of this conversation, Socrates describes why he first took up philosophy. What Socrates says is of considerable relevance to our current conceptions of philosophy, and to the relationship between philosophy and science.

He begins by recounting how, when he was young, he had 'an extraordinary passion for that branch of learning which is called natural science'. He thought that it would be marvellous to know the causes by which each thing comes and ceases and continues to be. So he occupied himself, much as our scientists do today, with asking how life comes about, how we think, what the brain has got to do with memory and knowledge, and with questions of physics and astronomy. After a while, though, he came to the conclusion that he was 'uniquely unfitted for this form of inquiry'.

In part this was because it seemed to make things which had seemed clear enough quite obscure, paradoxical even. So, far from explaining things, science simply seemed to confuse the seeker after truth. I do not know how far this is a legitimate criticism of science today. On the one hand science has been extraordinarily successful in helping us to manipulate the physical world, and to predict what is going to happen in all kinds of areas. But on the other, many of its theories and explanations remain extremely puzzling.

For all the myriad expositions, popular and advanced, do any of us really understand the theory of relativity? Can we really live with it? Time might have to be like it says, from the physical point of view, but can we really come to terms with the idea that there are different times for different observers? Or that whether two events are happening at the same time is a question which admits of no absolute answer outside the time-frames of specific observers, who may well give different answers about whether or not the same events are simultaneous?

Equally the paradoxes of quantum theory – the idea, for example, that if a particle has a definite position it has no momentum and vice versa – remain as puzzling and as unresolved as they did in the 1920s when they first emerged. If, as some physicists say, we just have to live with these and other obscurities in order to avail ourselves of the amazing predictive and manipulative power of these theories, then the extent to which science actually produces *understanding* could still be as open a question for us as it was for Socrates in the fifth century BC.

But the diet of paradoxes and obscurities produced by scientific reasoning was not Socrates' fundamental difficulty. His fundamental difficulty was that scientific explanations were not of the right type, for they did not explain things in terms of the ultimate reasons for things being as they were.

One day, though, he heard someone reading from a book by Anaxagoras (one of the so-called pre-Socratic philosophers). What Anaxagoras said was that it is Mind that produces order and is the cause of everything. 'Somehow it seemed right that Mind should be the cause of everything'; for Mind would be arranging every individual thing in the way that is best for it. In investigating this, Mind would also be finding out just what constituted the best for each individual thing and why it should be the best. We would also learn about the ultimate reason for the universe as a whole, and the order in it. And we would learn about what the best is for each individual person.

So, for example, Socrates thought that Anaxagoras would begin by informing us whether the earth was round or flat, and all kinds of other details about what it was and how things in it worked. Having done that, he would then go on to the really important task: that of showing in detail why it was better that it was flat or round (as the case may be). And so for everything else, including what constituted the best and highest good for each of us.

'It was a wonderful hope, my friend, but it was quickly dashed. As I read on I discovered that the fellow made no use of Mind and assigned to it no causality for the order of the world, but adduced causes like air and ether and water and many other absurdities.' This, says Socrates, would be as stupid as if someone were to try to explain what he, Socrates, was doing here in prison by talking about his bones and sinews, and the way bones are rigid and sinews contract and relax, and the way all these things had operated together to end up with him sitting here in a bent position.

An explanation of this sort would never mention the real reasons for his being in prison, in Athens. The real reasons are that Athens had thought it better to condemn him, and that he, for his part, had thought it better not to go into exile (which he could have done), but to stay and submit to whatever penalty Athens ordered. 'Because, by Dog, I fancy

that these sinews and bones would have been in the neigh-
bourhood of Megara or Boeotia long ago (impelled by a
conviction of what is best!) if I did not think that it was more
right and honourable to submit to whatever penalty my
country orders than to take to my heels and run away.'

Of course, Socrates adds, without his sinews and bones
he could not do what he thinks is best. But we have to
distinguish between the real cause, and that which is simply
the condition which enables the real cause to operate. And
that is Mind, acting for the best, both in his own case, and in
the case of the universe as a whole.

As literature, *Phaedo* is astonishing in its drama, its
flexibility and its imagery. The passage we have just been
looking at moves into a proof by Socrates of the immortality
of the soul, and then, inexorably, to the final scene of almost
unbearable pathos, in which he drinks the hemlock. In
reading it we share the reactions of his friends, and
understand something of Socrates' own sense of mission,
and why he thought that whatever befell the good man on
earth, deep down he could never be harmed. But what of the
philosophy underlying the poetry?

At first sight, for all its apparent simplicity of expression,
much of what Socrates says is hard for us to grasp. Do we
these days have any notion of someone who might think an
honourable death – on a trumped-up charge – was better
than exile, just because he owed his city a debt? And what of
the complaint about Anaxagoras? Do we really expect
scientists or even philosophers to tell us why the
dispositions of the moon and the planets and other physical
facts are for the best, as opposed to simply being as they are?

To which, if Stephen Hawking is anything to go by, the

answer is clearly no. In *A Brief History of Time* Hawking tells us that if we can discover why it is that we and the universe exist, then we would know the mind of God.[7] But the most he actually promises that science will ever be able to do is to construct a 'grand unified theory' of how things operate. If this theory was complete and covered every type of phenomenon, it would be a huge achievement. But it would be quite different from the sort of thing Socrates was looking for. It would be quite different from any ultimate reason for the existence of the universe itself, with all its law and particles and Big Bangs and so on. Nor would it show us that some Mind had had our existence in mind as part of his intention in creating or guiding the universe.

It is not just that science cannot answer ultimate 'Why?' questions of this sort. It is not clear that philosophy can, either, at least not so long as it sticks to what we can know by human reason alone. Does reason give us any conception of a supreme intelligence guiding and controlling everything for the best? Science, it seems, can get on perfectly well without any such idea. At least it has done for the past four or five centuries, the time of its most remarkable advances.

And the more we know of nature and the universe in general, the more doubtful it seems that there is any guiding intelligence. In too many ways nature seems far from perfect. There is too much suffering, too much imperfection, too much waste.

So perhaps the Mind which Socrates failed to find in Anaxagoras is, despite Socrates, just too ambitious a target even for philosophy. But let us go back to Socrates in his prison cell, and his sinews and bones. At that level, at the human level, questions about the best and acting for the best are central. They are central to the way we act and the way we think about ourselves and each other. And they cannot be reduced to talk about sinews and bones, or even to talk about neurons and brain processes.

Why am I sitting here writing this, when I could be out drinking with my friends, or watching a rugby match? Because I want to earn enough money to give my children a good upbringing. And why do I believe I have to do that? And what is a good upbringing anyway? No doubt in pursuing these questions I will have to talk about the duties of parenthood, and also about the type of upbringing and education which will provide a basis for human fulfilment.

All this is very much in the area of what we conceive to be the best and highest good, something on which the science of sinews and bones and the brain is silent.

For bones, sinews and even brains just act as they are caused to do by other physical or neurophysiological processes. They do not act because they think some things are more worth doing than others. They do not formulate ideas about the best form of life at all. So long as we stay on the level of the operations of bones, sinews and brains, all we will ever find are other movements of bones, sinews and brains, all equally deaf to thoughts about the best form of life.

Of course my actions and the reasons for them do not have to be particularly praiseworthy. Maybe in writing I am simply out to fulfil some ambition to out-perform a rival philosopher. But, even though unworthy, this is still a reason, which guides and moulds my activity. It is not the blind firing of bits of my brain, or the mechanical operation of my limbs and my nervous system. And as a reason, my ambition is in the sphere of reasons. It is the sort of thing which naturally raises questions about what is really worth acting on, about what is really good.

Anyone who has a child knows that this is so. You ask your son why he took the last cake, and he replies 'Because I wanted it.' And you say 'Was that a good thing to do when you had already had three, and your sister hadn't had any?'

What I want to suggest is that this giving and discussing of reasons is a fundamental aspect of human life. It is basic to the way we conceive of ourselves and others. We think of ourselves and of others very much in terms of the sorts of reasons we and they have for our actions. We discuss these reasons with each other, trying to bring others to our point of view, or being converted by others to theirs. Our assessments of character are very much based on the types of reasons people have for what they do, and their constancy or inconstancy in applying them.

We all believe that some reasons are better than others, according to some ultimate standard of goodness. We do not, for example, believe that it is mere whim that leads us to believe that honesty is good or that cruelty to children is a matter of indifference. The having of convictions of this sort is part of the very fabric of our lives. We could not even understand, let alone live with, people for whom beliefs of this sort were of no significance. (And we can say this, even while admitting that in principle some of our cherished principles were wrong; for admitting they might be *wrong* implies that some other principles are *right* – and not just arbitrary alternatives to our own.)

This giving and taking and defending of reasons is more fundamental to us as human beings than science. It is a critical part of every human life, part of what makes us human, whereas many people live lives in which science plays no part. But more fundamentally science itself, as a human activity, is something we do (or not) only because we think we have good reasons for doing it (or not). Science as an activity, then, depends on our having an idea of what it is good to do, an idea which includes the doing of science as a part. Without this notion there would be no science.

But even if science is part of the good life and worth pursuing for its own sake, for the sake of the truths it reveals about the world (as I believe to be the case), it is not science which shows us that this is so. For, as we have already shown, science tells us nothing about that which is good and that which is less good: for that we need philosophy. How, though, does this philosophy, this weighing and judging of reasons about what is the best, operate?

In a sense the answer to this question can only be fully understood once one has done some philosophy, and seen how it works. And it is also worth pointing out straight away that 'the best' which philosophy considers is not only the best in the sphere of morality. We can and should raise questions of a philosophical sort about 'the best' in knowledge, in aesthetics, in science itself, and much else besides.

We want to know just what we can actually know about the world, about whether there is true beauty in art or in nature, about whether science gives us a true account of nature – and about what might be meant by making claims in these areas. In reflecting on these things, we are doing philosophy. We are pushing questions about justification and truth and goodness back beyond our normal practices of making such judgements.

We are asking questions about the status of the practices themselves. Do they deliver what they seem to promise? And is what they promise worth striving for?

But even at the beginning, the question of method is unavoidable. What I hope will become apparent as we go on is that within our lives and practices as they are, we do have the resources to raise and answer the fundamental questions in which we are interested. What we need to do is to uncover those aspects of what we ordinarily do and think which are normally too obvious, too much taken for granted, but which, once brought into full view, can afford us the answers for which we are looking. It is this uncovering of and reasoning about basic aspects of our lives and practices which will be occupying us in the chapters which follow.

Some of the answers which this procedure suggests may at times seem surprising. But the surprises will not be those of science, which require a special language, a technical training and a special expertise to uncover, and which often assault common sense. As indicated in the previous chapter, there are styles of philosophy which do appear to share these characteristics of science; but from my point of view, that in itself is enough to awaken suspicion of both the style and the conclusions.

It is true that philosophy, properly conducted, requires concentration and effort, and also attention to argument and a degree of intellectual rigour. A sort of training is indeed necessary for these things, together with some knowledge of those works of the past which have been most significant in pursuing philosophical vision and argument; but this is not like the sort of training involved in learning how to operate scientific instruments and how to interpret scientific data.

Philosophical significance must, in the end, relate to universal human concerns and interests, and it must be such as to be available to anyone prepared to think. That too much philosophy today has all the defects of a typical academic specialism – jargon-laden, self-referential, pedantic, and of little interest to any non-professional – is not to its credit. And if, as Nietzsche said, we can trace the rise of academic philosophy back to Kant, the 'catastrophic spider', as Nietzsche called him, that is not to Kant's credit either, however much in fact Kant was actually pursuing some of the most basic philosophical concerns and however much his arguments and conclusions can, albeit with difficulty, be expressed in a generally intelligible form.

The arguments and conclusions to which philosophy directs us should, in the main, be accessible to anyone prepared to think about things they already know, and expressible in terms they already have. This is partly because the conclusions of philosophy have in the end to be justified in such terms, on the basis of the common experience of mankind, for that is all we have as a basis for judging about the highest and the best.

The common experience of mankind is not, as is sometimes claimed, simply a deposit of outdated myth and prejudice. It is rather that fertile and evolving culture which has enabled us to come to regard some myths and prejudices as outdated; it is also the soil from which particular branches of expertise, such as those of science, have sprung, and which sustains them. And it is, of course, true that some of our new forms of expertise have altered the common experience of mankind. They have closed off some possibilities for us and opened up others. But this is something we need to reflect on too, on whether in this opening and closing our lives have been enriched or narrowed. Once again our only resource for judging is what at the deepest level we think and feel, and which in the tumult of everyday life and its fashions may need philosophical reflection to bring to consciousness.

It is not just fashion and the noise of the everyday that philosophy can go behind. We live in an age dominated in many fields by experts. As we know from sometimes bitter experience, experts are notoriously bad at relating the fruits of their expertise to the wider human context in which they might be applied. Looking at particular expertises in the light of the best and highest good is very much part of philosophy's role today, just as it was in the time of Socrates.

Philosophy, then, reflects on the ultimate value and validity of some of our basic practices and beliefs. Despite the failures of twentieth-century philosophy, it can, as we will see, suggest some positive conclusions about the nature of ourselves and our abilities. And it can do this without relying on religious revelation or 'wisdom' in some quack sense. It can do it by reminding us of things which we already know and believe and act on, but which are at times obscured from us by intellectual fashions and also by our own insensitivity to what is before our eyes. It can also help us to explore the wider implications of particular branches of enquiry. Philosophy, even in the twenty-first century, can and should say something about the meaning of life.

But before we can make good any of these ambitious promises, we need to go back to the very beginning. Can we actually know anything at all? For if we can't, everything we say in philosophy and elsewhere will be built on sand.

3 So, What Then Can I Know?

The philosopher starts as an isolated individual. You look out on the world. There is you, the observer, the subject of experience. And, outside you there is everything else, the world and all its contents. These contents, of course, include other people and all their opinions and beliefs. These opinions and beliefs differ widely among themselves, a positive cacophony of views. So what, then, can we know? What can *I* know?

Modern philosophy – that is, philosophy since the sixteenth century – has been preoccupied with this question, understandably enough given that during the sixteenth and seventeenth centuries wars were fought over the truth or falsity of beliefs. This was also the period in which science seemed to be making decisive breaks with the past and overturning long-held and cherished beliefs.

So we saw Montaigne, the French nobleman, retiring to a tower on his estate, and reviving ancient scepticism. We could really know nothing. All was opinion – and opinion, even one's own, was constantly changing. All was relative to one's point of view. We could make our way around the world, just about, through the information given to us by our senses. But that told us nothing about the ultimate validity of what we believed, or about the true essence of the world.

Science, which claimed to give us ultimate truth, suffered from the same variability and controversy as did other areas of enquiry. Our beliefs tell us only how things seem to be, not what they are. On anything more than seeming, we should remain in peaceful silence, waiting on God's grace to enlighten us.

Then there was Francis Bacon, the English statesman, more optimistic than Montaigne in that he believed in the possibilities of the new science. But these possibilities would be realized only if we cleared out of our minds all the clutter of past beliefs and prejudices. We had to see the world afresh with eyes innocent of any thought or theorizing. But what Bacon did not explain was how, without some ideas about what it was we were looking at or for, we could make any sense of the confusing multitudes of information our senses are assaulted with at any moment. We also need some ideas about when our senses actually are reliable, and when they are likely to mislead us.

To see both these points, close your eyes for a moment and then, on opening them, try to explain what it is you are seeing without assuming what you already believe about the types of objects there are. What you will be confronted with is a confusing jumble – a buzzing, booming confusion, as William James put it – without any focus or clarity. Then, further, in making any sort of sense of our experience, we make all kinds of assumptions about distances and about perspective. We also assume we know about the differences between real things and those features of our visual experience which are merely produced by optical distortions. These include such things as shadows and sticks appearing bent in water. Then there are the parallel lines which meet in the distance, the mountains that look blue, the moon which follows the walker over the roof-tops, and much else besides.

But it is not just that we bring assumptions to our experience. As Montaigne had argued, all these illusions weaken the trust we might initially and naïvely have that our senses are reliable sources of knowledge.

René Descartes, the great French mathematician and philosopher, concluded that the whole of knowledge needed new foundations.[8] He retired from the fighting of the Thirty Years War to a stove-heated room to think things out afresh on his own. He resolved to accept nothing of which he could not be absolutely sure.

Following Montaigne, Descartes was well aware of optical and other illusions. He was aware of the ways in which our perceptions of colour, sound, taste and smell seem highly dependent on very variable features of ourselves and of the environment, such as the time of day, the food I have eaten and much else besides. There is also the intriguing bucket of water into which I put my hands. To the hand which was previously cold the water seems hot, while to the hand which has been warming over a fire it seems cold. So is the same water both hot and cold?

All these cases cast doubt on the reliability of the senses. But Descartes' questioning went a lot deeper. How many times, he asks, have I believed myself to be doing this and that, seated as he was when writing before the fire, and then woken up and realized that it was all a dream? How do I know that I am not dreaming now?

Of course, I might say that I would carry out the usual tests and precautions in such a case. I might pinch myself, walk around, speak to other people. Indeed I might. But – can I be sure that I am not dreaming that I am doing all this? My very attempt to show to myself that this experience I am having now is not a dream could actually be part of a dream itself.

If I cannot tell whether I am dreaming or not, then my senses must be very unreliable indeed. It seems that the experiences I have in a dream – and which are wholly illusory – are no different from those I have in my waking state. So those might be just as illusory as dream experiences as far as the real world is concerned.

But worse is to follow. Descartes believed that even in a dream there are some things I could still be sure of. I could still be sure that 2 + 3 = 5, or that a triangle had three sides or that all physical objects had some extension. I can be sure of these things because they carry their proof with them. If I understand what it is to be 2 and 3 and plus, then I must get 5. If I know what a physical object is, I will see that it must have some shape and size.

Or must these things be so? It is true that we human beings cannot imagine any alternative. But suppose that our minds are out of kilter with reality? That they have been constructed by an evil demon to misrepresent reality in a systematic way?

Descartes' evil-demon hypothesis may seem quaint, but he is touching on a genuine problem. How do we know that what we can and can't think (imagine, believe) is of ultimate significance. Mightn't our minds just be too feeble or deluded to cope with how things really are? (Perhaps this is at the root of our difficulties in understanding quantum theory and relativity.)

The dreaming and evil-demon arguments have been given a modern incarnation, which raises much the same questions. These days we believe that our experiences and our thoughts are dependent on the state of our brains. So let us suppose that a brain is taken out of its owner's body, and kept alive in a vat. It is wired up by mad scientists in such a way that it receives the same impulses from machines devised by the scientist as a normal brain does from its body, limbs and sense organs.

The brain in the vat would have the same flow of experience as a normal embodied person making his or her way around the world. How do I know that *I* am not that brain? Nothing in my experience could show me that I am not, because by definition the flows of experience are identical. So could I actually be a brain in a vat? How could I tell that I was not?

Descartes solved his problems in the following way. I might really be dreaming. My thought processes might be under the control not of reality but of the evil demon. But even in these circumstances, there is one thing I could not be deceived about. I could not be deceived about the fact that I am now thinking. Even if I am in a state of total doubt, as Descartes was himself in his stove-heated room, I am still thinking. Even if I am being deceived in all my thoughts, I am still thinking those thoughts. And if I am thinking, then I exist. *Cogito, ergo sum*: I think, therefore I am.

But what – apart from being a thinking thing – am I? Am I an embodied human being? Or am I a disembodied dreamer? Or a brain in a vat? Descartes believed that he could prove that he was an embodied human being. He thought that he could prove God's existence and that a good

God would not make us subject to the illusion we all share that we are embodied persons in a real world if that were not true. But most philosophers then and since have been less convinced by Descartes' positive arguments than by the power of his scepticism. The search was on to show how we could move from the fact of our experience, which we could not doubt, to the justification of our all-too-vulnerable beliefs about the world which we take our experience to be experience of.

What Descartes had shown was that while we could not doubt that we were having an experience of some sort, we could always doubt that the world outside our experience was as it seemed to be. We could also doubt what we were in ourselves, apart from the bare fact of being a subject of experience of some sort.

An immediate reaction to all this was to argue that many of our experiences are as they were because they are being caused by things outside us. We have an experience of a tree, for example, because a tree is causing the experience. Of course this explanation would not do when the experience was, dream-like, caused only by things inside us. And many of our experiences are of our internal workings. But many are not, and of those it seems reasonable to suppose that they are as they are because of the things which cause them. So my current visual experience is of a tree and not of a dog because there is a tree interacting with my eyes and not a dog.

But how do we know that my experience of the tree truly represents the tree? That the tree is indeed how it looks to me? How do I know that all kinds of things in my visual experience of the tree are not being added by me and my sense organs? Maybe the tree's colour is something I bring to the world. Maybe the world, including the tree, consists ultimately of colourless particles (as Newton believed). In Newton's account the impression of colour is just what is produced when those colourless particles start interacting with my eyes, and through them with my brain.

The trouble is that we cannot step outside our experience and view the tree directly, so as to compare the real thing with how it appears to us. The 'real thing' always comes to us via the medium of our experience.

We can imagine other creatures whose experience of the same world is quite different from our own, and not just the Martians and extraterrestrials of science fiction. What about bats, whose substitute for sight appears to be echo-location (however that might be experienced by them)? What about dogs, with their super-developed sense of smell and blindness to colour? We might say that our experience is more truthful than that of these other creatures; but mightn't they, with as much right, say the same about us?

Even if the world is as it appears to us, how can we be sure that the regularities which have been so marked a feature of our experience up to now will continue in the future? On what grounds can we rule out the alarming possibility that the future might be very different from the past? This worry is the so-called problem of induction, and it is not, on the face of it, a purely theoretical possibility. After all, in many ways things do change as time goes on.

So what is to stop them changing in ways we cannot predict, and which may have disastrous effects on our very existence? In living and planning our lives we require confidence that the world will go on pretty much as it has in the past. We do not expect planes to fall out of the sky or bridges to collapse. We expect food to continue to nourish and fire to burn, and so on. Without these and many, many other expectations continuing to be fulfilled, life would be impossible. Yet do we have any proof of any of this, as opposed to a blind hope?

So even if we are not dreaming or brains in vats, we seem to be faced with some stiff challenges to our claims to know what the world outside us is really like. And what about the world inside? Although I might be sure that I am thinking now, does this take me any further than the present moment? Is the 'I' which thinks now the same as the 'I' which thought in the past? And will I be the same person in the future?

In many ways I am not the same as I was: thank goodness, some might say. There is no constant thread which unites all my experiences. Maybe it is just an illusion that even at this moment I am one united self. Perhaps in me there is just an incoherent mass of warring and conflicting thoughts, desires, motives, emotions, beliefs and unconscious urges with nothing really tying them all together. The idea that there is an essential me, a self, a soul which persists through all my thoughts and experiences is one of our most cherished beliefs. But much of what 'I' do is hardly conscious at all. 'I' can seem as divided as I am united. My beliefs about my own motives and feelings may be as much a product of self-deception as of unclouded, accurate insight into my inner psyche.

So, what am I? What can I know? I can know that I am having some experiences, but not that they faithfully represent the world. I cannot know whether I am awake or dreaming. I might be a brain in a vat, manipulated and deceived by mad scientists. Even if there is a world, it might cease to be as it has been. And 'I' might be no more than a succession of loosely connected and often conflicting experiences, with nothing substantial above or below them.

Such, anyway, would be the picture yielded by one type of philosophical attempt to found all our beliefs on firm ground. But, far from finding firm ground, we are sinking in a quicksand. All we can cling to is the vanishing point of momentary experience. We have that, but we have nothing else – no world, no self, no foundations.

But perhaps it was a mistake to think that we could base anything on a retreat to inner experience. And perhaps, in the retreat, we are working with a misleading idea of experience. Maybe, having gone through these stages of scepticism, we should start again from a different point.

4 Myself and Other Persons

The scepticism which has been so marked a feature of philosophy since the time of Descartes has a very particular view of experience. It assumes that the philosopher is an isolated intelligence, cut off from the world. As such he or she passively receives all kinds of stimulation and experience. But he or she is allowed no sense of the nature of this flow of experience or where it has come from or how it has come about. He or she then has to construct or justify the everyday conception of life and the world without going beyond this private, disconnected stream of experience.

Not surprisingly, this cannot be done: the basis for construction is just too flimsy. The distance between this thinned-out experience and how the world actually presents itself to us is just too great.

Philosophy, then, seems forever locked into scepticism and even into the extreme form of scepticism known as solipsism. This is the view that there is just me, an experiencer locked, as it were, into my own private cinema of experience. My screen of images constantly rolls, as do the CD-roms with the information for my other senses. But beyond that I know nothing. I might be a brain in a vat. All that makes my real life possible is mere conjecture, clothed with doubt and uncertainty, consigned to the dustbin of stone-age thought.

Of course we know that we cannot live like that: and so do the philosophers. They say that we live by 'animal belief', the unthinking assumptions about the physical world, the future and other people which make living possible. But philosophy is no help here. It seems to be able to provide no support for our unthought and naïve, 'animal' beliefs, as Hume called them: the presuppositions we cannot do without, but which philosophy shows to be baseless.

But what is the use of a philosophy we cannot live by? And what if this philosophy falsifies the very experience it takes to be our sole source of certainty?

For, when we really examine our experience without philosophical preconceptions, we see that it is not at all like the picture we have been working with. In the first place, we are not the passive receivers of experience beloved of philosophical legend. We do not simply absorb the images and other sensations we are given on the sceptical account. We are not like some paralysed person, strapped to his chair, in a cinema of experience over which he can exercise no direct control; or even less a brain in a vat, at the mercy of whatever the mad scientists throw at us.

From the start we are active in the world. The quality of our experience is that of an agent, of a being who acts. It is in our acting and moving around our environment that we modify and determine how we experience things. We do this all the time, and unreflectively.

And we do it not by some mysterious exercise of thought. We do it by moving our limbs, by touching things and by feeling resistance. We move in for a better look at something to convince ourselves that we are seeing accurately. We change the angle of view and the vantage point. Outside the unreal worlds of dreaming and of the cinema and the television our perception is always intermingled with action, with movement, with handling things and with changes of position on our part.

In short, the passive reception of sensations, cut off from activity in the world, on which so much philosophical scepticism rests, is a myth. And so is the gap between our sense experience and the world which we take that experience to be experience of, because when we understand our experience correctly there is no gap to bridge. There is simply the world, and us moving around in it, experiencing it in and through our movement in it and interaction with it.

What we are considering here is the primitive, given, felt quality of experience. Right from the start, our experience is already rooted in activity in a real world which is not of our making, and to which our desires and thoughts have to conform, as we quickly realize from our earliest infancy onwards. To be sure, it is still possible for someone to insist that he or she might be a brain in a vat or the subject of some other cruel delusion.

But given that any such suggestion would fly in the face of all that our experience naturally suggests, the burden of proof lies with the doubter. How could it be that things are so utterly different from how they appear? How could the, as it were, 'en-worlded' quality of experience be so wrong? Especially when, unlike the sequences of dreams or films, our normal everyday expectations of the world, based on that experience, are confirmed over and over again in pretty well everything we do and think?

By 'our normal everyday expectations of the world', I

mean things like the assumption that the ground beneath my feet won't give way as I walk, the assurance that the table in my room will still be there when I return and won't have dissolved into a heap of dust, the faith that the sun will rise tomorrow and the paper be on the doormat, and so on. When one thinks about it, one sees that everyday life depends on countless such assumptions, and that everyday life also confirms the vast majority of them.

Saying that our expectations are confirmed over and over again in our life in the world tells us something about the fit between our experience and beliefs and the world. It tells us that we are not unadapted to the conditions in which we find ourselves. Our sense organs deliver information on which we can rely. Our basic beliefs and thoughts are not wholly erroneous. All this is important, and we will return to it.

But the continual confirmation of our expectations also tells us something important about the world. It tells us that the world is not chaotic. It follows regular patterns which make the having and confirming of expectations possible.

Now, in one sense there is no necessity that the world should be like this. Perhaps even in this universe there are some places far more chaotic than the planet earth. Maybe in the future the earth will descend into a type of randomness which will make human life impossible.

If this were to happen, it would also make coherent thought and belief impossible, for coherent thought and belief depend on the ability to distinguish within one's experience between those passages of experience one takes to be genuine and those which one takes to be illusory. But in the experience a conscious being had in a largely random world, there would be no effective contrast between the orderly sequences of normal experience and the disconnected, irrational and disjointed passages characteristic of dreams, hallucinations and drug-induced trances.

In such a world we would be unable to distinguish waking from dreaming. We would actually be in the situation which, for philosophical purposes, Descartes erroneously imagined we might be in. Still, insofar as life and experience are possible, the world, or at least the bits of it we inhabit, must be regular and law-like. That is to say, it must follow regularities which we can see as the laws governing the way things have to happen.

So we can say that the vase had to fall to the ground because the boy knocked it off the table, that the paper had to burn once it was in the fire, that the tree had to die because it was deprived of water. We can say these and many other similar things because we know that these are the ways that things happen in our world, and are bound to happen unless we do something to interfere with the normal course of nature. Sometimes we can interfere. We may be able to catch the vase and stop it falling, or save the paper by putting the fire out, or give the tree water. But acting in these ways assumes that there is a normal pattern to things, that we know what that pattern is, and that we know the normal ways of effectively interfering with it.

What does all this say about us? It says that we ourselves are material beings, embodied and living in a material world, knowing and understanding something about it. As a material being, I too am subject to the laws and regularities of nature. I am a product of nature, produced by natural processes and relying on natural processes for my survival.

No doubt, too, I am a product of ages of biological development, through the processes of evolution. My instincts and many of my desires are rooted in my evolutionary history. Others are due to my particular psychological make-up, and others again to my social circumstances.

For just as I am revealed in my most primitive experience as being embodied, so in my thinking and acting am I revealed as being surrounded by other people, and depending on them in all sorts of ways. Who I think myself to be, the language I speak, even the thoughts and aspirations I can have: all are clearly dependent on my birth, my upbringing and on those with whom fate brings me into contact. Even my ability to think and express sceptical thoughts depends on my having a language in which to formulate such ideas, and on my belonging to a tradition and a culture in which they have been explored.

We thus avoid the impasse of scepticism by emphasizing the rootedness of experience both in the material world, and also in the social world (of which we have not yet said much, but which will play an increasingly important role as we go on). But is there a cost in emphasizing our materiality and our sociality in this way? Do we avoid scepticism only by making ourselves a part of nature, as much governed by nature's laws and regularities as any other part? And if we are social beings through and through, does it mean that what we think and do are constrained by our social background? If so, what becomes of human freedom? For if we are products of nature and society, can we be free? Can we aspire to anything more than an existence limited by the facts of our nature and the horizons of our society?

Here, though, the existence of philosophical questioning and even scepticism points to something about us which is as important as our rootedness in the material and social worlds. For we are not simply bound by those worlds. We can ask questions of a fundamental sort about the truth of what we think we know. We can, like Socrates, ask about what it is best that should be done.

And in asking questions about truth and goodness in these ways we are simply not bound by the limitations of our origins. At the limit we will be asking about the status of the very assumptions given to us in nature and by our upbringing. We can, as we saw in considering scepticism, put into question all our beliefs. We can, as we saw with Socrates, try to get behind conventional notions of goodness to what is really and ultimately good.

In pursuing these lines of questioning we may, as in the case of scepticism, come to validate our original commonsense conceptions. A Socratic enquiry into goodness may bring us back to things we have, in a sense, known all along. But even if this is so, in the return to common sense and to what we have known all along, we will have attained a higher viewpoint than that from which we began. We will also be in a good position to rebut those who seek to dismiss or ridicule the common experience of mankind.

But how, it will be asked, can we escape the limits of our origins just by thinking? Won't our thinking itself be constrained by the same limits as the thinkers in their bodily and social origins? How, by mere thought, can we ascend to a more universal, a more ultimate viewpoint? Won't we be forever held prisoner by the limits of our conceptions and the restrictions of what, in our society and in our language, we can think?

To see how thought is not and cannot be a cage imprisoning thinkers, we need to reflect on the nature of thought itself. Let us begin by considering the simple demand that in thinking we do not contradict ourselves.

The reason why we should not contradict ourselves is because if we do, we will simply lapse into incoherence. You cannot, for example, think both that it is five o'clock in the afternoon and not five o'clock in the afternoon. The one thought cancels the other out. You end up thinking nothing. There is no thought. In symbolic terms, you cannot think both p and not-p.

Now this law of non-contradiction, as it is called, is nothing specific to English or French or Chinese. Nor is it anything about how English or French or Chinese people actually think. It is about a pre-condition of all thought – any thinking, in whatever language or culture. It is prior to any particular thought. It transcends all particular thoughts. It governs all thinking.

It is similar to the rules which specify what follows from what, the so-called rules of inference. Suppose that it is true that Socrates is a man, and it is also true that if Socrates is a man, then he is mortal. Then it must be true that Socrates is mortal. In symbolic form, if I believe p, and if q follows from p, then on pain of contradiction, I must believe q too.

Similarly, if Saturn is a planet and does not move in a circle, it cannot be the case that if anything is a planet, it therefore moves in a circle. If p implies q and q is not true, then p cannot be true either. This is a very important form of inference, for it is used in showing how particular observations (in this case, the non-circular orbit of Saturn) are used to falsify theories which are postulated in science (in this case, that all planets move in circles); but once again the rule is of quite general application, and is used whenever particular facts are used to test the truth of general principles.

Once again there is nothing here which is peculiar to any particular language or society. We are talking about truths which govern all thought in whatever language or form. Without principles or rules of the sort we have been examining (and which, of course, include many more examples than those we have just examined) neither thought nor language is conceivable.

It is true that we need a language to think and express thoughts of any complexity, and to develop arguments. But behind and beyond any language are the rules which govern argument and which make language capable of expressing coherent thought. While I might learn these rules through speaking a particular language and living in a particular community, once learned, I can use them to criticize and evaluate uses and practices prevalent in my own linguistic community.

This criticism and evaluation of our thought and practice is not confined to its purely structural or logical elements. We can also examine, criticize and, if necessary, change any beliefs we hold as individuals, or which are prevalent in our community more generally.

It is a striking, though insufficiently remarked fact that our language, as any natural language, is highly flexible and plastic. Far from being a prison constraining thought, English, like all natural languages, enables us to express and entertain the opposite of what we actually believe. Further, although we learn particular words and ideas in specific contexts, once learned they can be applied and thought about in new contexts, quite different from those in which they were learned.

It is this possibility which enables us to tell stories, and also to speculate about things being quite different from how we initially conceive them. And that possibility in turn is what makes philosophy – the rational evaluation of belief and practice – possible.

Of course in evaluating and belief or a practice, I will be using particular standards of truth and judgement. In using the ones I do use, I will no doubt be making assumptions which I do not challenge at the time. Some may be erroneous and simply the product of a particular culture or context. But in conducting my evaluations, I will be aiming at what is true, pure and simple. It is this thought which guides my thinking and makes sense of it. If I realize that one of my assumptions is just an artefact of a particular culture or environment and not valid generally, I am already on the road to dispensing with it. In replacing it I will be looking for a principle which does take us closer to our goal – truth itself, unmixed with local quirks and fancies.

Do I ever have a guarantee that I have reached the truth pure and simple? In the case of logical principles, like the law of non-contradiction, I surely do. Such principles form the first and the last word of any intellectual activity whatever. There is no going beyond or behind them. Because they are the presuppositions of any coherent thought whatever, their falsity is, quite simply, inconceivable.

Things are less straightforward when we come to beliefs

about how the world happens to be or about what is good or worthwhile. We can always entertain the thought that the world might be very different from how we believe it to be or that what we believe to be wrong might actually be quite right after all. We do not lapse into incoherence here in the way we would if we denied the law of non-contradiction and other basic logical principles.

And yet . . . as we have already suggested in the case of scepticism, the mere possibility of the opposite is not in itself a good reason for abandoning a belief, particularly not if that belief has survived both time and critical evaluation. For we are never simply passive recipients of beliefs in either factual or moral realms. In holding a belief we are holding it to be true. It is not something that just happens to us with no need for reflection on our part. Insofar as we do reflect on what we believe, we challenge it, we submit it to scrutiny; we test it against the demands of truth. We take it out of the flow of life, so to speak, and focus on its truth or falsity, as it is in itself. The falsity of a well-tested, long-lasting and well-examined belief may not be inconceivable, but we always have to ask ourselves whether its falsity would be more incredible than its truth.

In examining and certifying our beliefs in this sort of way, we will be demonstrating both in theory and practice that we are not condemned to an uncritical acceptance of whatever we are brought up to think or learn. We will be suggesting that we can test what we think we know against standards of truth with some claim to be thought objective. And objectivity will be increased to the extent that we can get others from different backgrounds and points of view to agree. For we will be showing that what we think or believe is not something which seems true to people from only one background or perspective.

So, in the testing of beliefs and ideals we can transcend their and our origins. But so, in a significant way, do we in thinking about them.

It is true that the thoughts and ideas we have, come to us first in particular circumstances. I first learn what a dog is in encountering a particular dog, and very likely in being exposed to the English word 'dog'. But once I have the idea of what a dog is, my thoughts about dogs are not confined to one particular dog, neither do they have to be expressed by means of the English word. I can think about dogs by using words of other languages, or by using different English words, or even by using no words at all.

Plato believed that in our thinking we gained access to another, abstract realm, far removed from this material world of change and decay, and far more perfect than it. Our thoughts were really about perfect forms, from which things on earth derived their meaning and significance. And in thinking, we could judge against absolute standards of truth, of goodness and of beauty with which we were acquainted before our birth, and with which we remained in life intermittently and fitfully in contact.

Full-blooded Platonism, as it is called, seemed to many even at the time to be exaggerated. Nonetheless, Plato was right in drawing attention to what might be called the freedom of thought. We can think and reason about things of which we have no experience. We can submit our thoughts to test and scrutiny. As we see dramatically in the case of arithmetic and geometry, but not exclusively there, ideas and thoughts, once formulated, develop in unexpected ways, as when Pythagoras demonstrated that the square on the hypotenuse of a right-angled triangle was equal to the sum of the squares on the other two sides. This proof was implicit in the idea of a right-angled triangle, but was not obvious or even envisaged before the proof.

We can also think of our thoughts as independent of any particular expression, as when Pythagoras expounded his proof in ancient Greek, a teacher explains it in English and a schoolchild copies it down in a book. Same thought, three very different expressions. And we also think of all thought as being subject to the same logical rules of universal application. In all these ways, thought and thinking seem only loosely connected to its actual physical expressions – written, spoken, and in all kinds of different languages, natural and artificial.

True as all this is, we are not pure intelligences, neither can we aspire to be, whatever Plato may have hoped. We are still creatures with a physical nature and a particular history and culture, even though none of this constrains us totally. What we must seek in philosophy is a *via media*, a middle way between a purely materialistic conception of ourselves and one which sees us as wholly malleable, bound only by the limits of what we can think or imagine.

It is clearly important to emphasize both the initial embedding of our thought and experience in the physical world and the extent to which we can break free of this embedding, if we are able to resist scepticism and relativism. Both these are disabling conditions, philosophically and morally. We can resist scepticism because we see that it is untrue to our most primitive and fundamental experience, which is of us acting and moving in a world with an existence apart from us. We can resist the relativistic thought that we are forever trapped in a limited and subjective view of the world because we see that some of our thought rests on foundations whose validity is unquestionable, and that in thinking about ourselves and our beliefs we can free ourselves from our limited starting points.

On the other hand there are dangers in thinking that we can do and think anything we like. It is perhaps no coincidence that Plato was at the same time philosophy's greatest advocate of thought's freedom from its material basis and the first and still most radical would-be reconstructor of society. Plato believed that by pure thought he could devise a social set-up which would be ideal, and also that this ideal society would be run by the power of unsullied philosophical thought. The rulers would be philosophers, trained for many years in the philosophical method, and they would legislate according to purely rational principles.

In Plato's ideal society,[9] although the lower orders would live lives of ordinary humanity, the rulers – the philosopher kings – would live in a way specifically designed to wean them from any normal human motivation. They would be strictly segregated from the rest of society. They would own no property. They would not be paid. They would breed in a random fashion decided by lot. Children would be brought up in common, and would not know who their parents were. There would be strict equality of the sexes. Art, music and religion would be subject to strict control to ensure that there was no room for deviant emotions, doctrines or displays.

Plato's conception of the state as a combination of armed

camp and primitive communism has proved endlessly fascinating to utopian reformers throughout the ages. Rather less so, one fancies, to those poor human beings forced to live – and die – under such regimes, from Calvin's Geneva to Lenin's Russia, to Hitler's Germany, to Mao's China. And that surely is the point. What Vaclav Havel called the 'scandalous chaos of life and its mysterious fertility' is resistant to the plans of ideologues. More to the point, human nature itself is not entirely flexible.

In the twentieth century the most dramatic and disastrous attempts to re-mould humanity were in the political sphere. We will never be entirely free from the temptation to think that a radical political blueprint might be better than the *status quo*. Still, a century of failed totalitarian experiments serves as a frightful warning.

Where we are far more likely to want to reform humanity is in the medical, genetic and social sphere. We have the power, or soon will, to re-draw the facts of conception and birth, to eliminate all kinds of abnormalities by genetic means, to choose the babies we want when we want, to institute all kinds of new sexual and familial arrangements, and to arrange our deaths as we choose. Reason, through the powers afforded us by science, is about to transform the brute facts of human biology and the traditional values based on those facts.

It is not simply human nature which is under assault in unprecedented ways. In all kinds of ways humanity seems to be recasting the natural world, and re-drawing our relationship with it. If we were simply intelligences, with no roots in the natural world, there might be no harm in any of this. But, the lessons of political revolution aside, the feeling persists that, for all our reason and freedom of thought, we human beings are products of nature. We rely on nature. Nature has formed us in all kinds of ways. In assaulting nature, we assault ourselves. In too radical a transformation of our own nature, we will unleash forces we cannot control and we will eradicate those natural feelings which give us some foundations for our lives and affections.

Is it possible to hold in balance the complex thought that we are part of the natural world and subject to historical constraints and limitations with the apparently unlimited possibilities afforded us by our thinking and intelligence? This question will occupy us in the next chapter.

5 Nature, Society and Individual

What, then, is human nature? Does it constrain us in what we can do and think? Should it?

In one very obvious sense we *are* constrained by nature: we have all kinds of purely physical limitations. But even here matters are not entirely clear. We can circumvent some of nature's limitations, and it often seems good that we should do so. No doubt many of us would have died without medical surgery or drugs. There are few who complain about that, or reject it on grounds of unnaturalness.

So, suppose we can re-draw the map of human birth, so that children could be conceived without sexual intercourse and without having to spend nine months in their mother's womb, what would be wrong with that? It would in many ways be far more convenient than nature's way, particularly for women who wanted to develop careers and for an economy which depended on women working. Surely this is just the sort of thing we should be able to choose to do if – as seems likely – medical developments can make it possible.

In any case, we do not simply face nature raw, either individually or collectively. Between each of us and nature, there is culture and history. And in culture and history there are all kinds of random and fortuitous results, outcomes and institutions, which could very easily have been different, and which actually are different in societies other than our own. We also know that many things which we take for granted in our lives, such as our nationality or our political arrangements, are things which are the result of historical processes only a few hundred years old.

Being English or British or American or part of a democratic or monarchical system are not natural facts, but artefacts of some highly questionable and even disreputable events and decisions far closer to us in time than we unthinkingly imagine. So aren't these also things which we should feel free to change as and when we wish?

The two most influential philosophical approaches to questions of this sort would see little wrong in revising political, moral or even biological facts as opportunity arises and as reason or convenience suggests.

The first of these is utilitarianism, that is the view that what really counts is the removal of avoidable suffering and the promotion of pleasure or happiness. Moreover, according to utilitarianism, in deciding what to do in any specific case, all that we should take into account are the amounts of pleasure and pain produced by a given action. If the pleasure outweighs the pain, then that is what we should do.

So if by experimenting on embryos we can cure some terrible affliction such as cancer, or prevent it altogether, then we should do so. Even if the embryos suffer pain – which is doubtful – the suffering of the comparative few needed for the experiments will be greatly outweighed by the benefits to all those mature human beings who will in the future be spared cancer.

Utilitarianism would also, in certain circumstances,

recommend practices such as abortion, euthanasia and even the killing of severely handicapped babies. The circumstances are those in which the pain of the life or lives affected greatly outweigh any benefits from living the life in question. Is it right, the utilitarian would say, to bring into the world a person who will be condemned to a life of extreme pain and an inevitable early death? Why prolong the life of an elderly person who has lost all dignity and most mental faculty?

Nor would utilitarians have any truck with the maintenance of social or political arrangements where these stand in the way of the increase of pleasure. Although such things are admittedly difficult to quantify, the utilitarian direction in these matters is clear enough. There is no point in hanging on to some institution or tradition simply because it is old or venerable: such an attitude would be anti-progressive and irrational.

Even from this briefest of sketches it soon becomes clear that utilitarianism faces some severe difficulties. One advantage of the utilitarian approach appears to be that it offers a decision procedure. It tells us in any situation what is the best thing to do. Unfortunately, this proves to be something of an illusion. It is easy to see that saving a drowning child will bring about more pleasure and eliminate more pain than my continuing my walk along the river-bank.

But what about the sort of question with which politicians are frequently confronted, as to whether, for example, it is better to spend public money on promoting the arts or providing kidney machines, or should a by-pass be driven through some unspoilt heath in order to relieve pressure on an historic town? How can you measure the gains and losses in each? Can they be compared at all? It looks as if we need some fuller account of the good life than utilitarianism can provide so long as it confines itself to generalized talk of pleasure and pain.

The question of the comparability of different types of pleasures and pains, different types of happiness and unhappiness was well known to the early utilitarian philosophers, Jeremy Bentham and John Stuart Mill. Bentham (notoriously) said that, other things being equal, if it produced more pleasure the trivial game of pushpin was to be preferred to poetry. The high-minded Mill demurred. Better, he said, to be Socrates dissatisfied than a fool satisfied, a man dissatisfied than a pig satisfied.[10]

Mill's point was that the higher one aimed, the greater the chance of disappointment. So if you valued the achievement, you should be willing to risk the pain of failure. True though this is, the conclusion of most commentators on Mill is that from within a utilitarian perspective, such matters are extremely difficult to decide, which prompts the thought that we need more than considerations of pleasure and pain in order to evaluate them.

But the non-comparability of goods is not utilitarianism's only problem or even its most taxing one. So long as morality is seen simply in terms of adding pleasures and subtracting pains, it looks as if majorities are entitled to exploit minorities. If 99 people get an awful lot of pleasure from torturing a cat or teasing some simple-minded child (who may not even realize what is happening) wouldn't it be right to do it on utilitarian grounds?

We do not need to take examples of obviously unpleasant

behaviour being enjoyed to make the point. Suppose that by reluctantly torturing the innocent child of a terrorist, we could discover when and where a bomb was to be planted, should we do it? Utilitarianism would almost certainly say that we should, given that we might thereby save dozens of lives and limbs. While some would agree, at least in practice, I think that many others would be uneasy. Doesn't the child have rights? Can it ever be right to torture anyone? Are we justified in harming an innocent person as a means to some other end, however good?

The main challenge to utilitarianism comes from what are known as rights-based theories. Where utilitarians sum pleasures and pains over all the individuals affected by a particular action or policy, rights theorists believe that morality must begin and end by preserving the rights of individuals. Rights may not be infringed, whatever the potential gain for the community as a whole. We are to treat individuals as ends, to be respected for themselves. Individuals are never to be used as means to other ends, however worthy. So it would always be wrong to torture an innocent person, even to extract information vital for security. Equally it would be completely wrong to use someone else's pain as a means to my pleasure or amusement.

In certain obvious ways, rights-based theories capture some of our basic moral intuitions more effectively than utilitarianism. They give voice to a very widespread sense that there are some ways we simply should not treat others, whatever the benefits. They also underpin the commonly accepted sense of the inalienable value of the individual. They describe a type of society most of us would find preferable to one run on utilitarian principles. In this rights-based society, the lives and freedoms of individuals will be seen as sacred.

Problems, though, remain. Where do these inalienable individual rights come from? And how far do they extend? It is easy to say that everyone has a right to life, liberty and the pursuit of happiness, but what do these things mean in practice, once we go beyond the most basic prohibitions on depriving others of their lives or property?

Can I do anything I want, provided it does not infringe someone else's rights? Can I commit suicide or collect child pornography? Can a pregnant woman dispose of an unwanted foetus on the grounds that it is part of her body? Or does the foetus have rights over the mother?

Do I have the right to keep whatever I earn or inherit? In which case – as some rights theorists claim – taxation to pay for such things as the education of other people's children or the medical treatment of the poor is a form of theft. Or do the rights of needy people mean that the rest of us have a duty to support them, however feckless and irresponsible they have been? Does my right to life mean that someone else might have to forgo his right to his own property in order to provide for me?

Do I have the right to freedom of speech, or do other people have the right not to hear things they find offensive? Do women have the right to join the armed forces, or men to paternity leave? Do homosexuals have the right to civil marriage and to having children? Do children have the right to divorce themselves from their parents if they feel their parents are damaging their self-esteem?

Faced with such questions, and with the increasingly strident claims of conflicting rights claimants, we may want to ask just what rights are. Where do they come from? How are particular rights claims to be justified? Bentham, that most forthright of first utilitarians, referred to rights as 'nonsense on stilts'; not only followers of Bentham might feel that a great deal of rights talk is simply a way of making one's demands on the rest of society sound more respectable.

Be that as it may, even this brief foray into controversies over rights suggests that no more than utilitarianism is rights talk hospitable to past institutions and traditions. Indeed, much of the contemporary demand for radical reform of past institutions and traditions comes from the sense that all too often such things have stood in the way of full human rights. Hence the demands for bills of rights; hence too the increasing tendency of people to go to the courts to pursue what they take to be their rights.

Rights talk and utilitarianism share an important presupposition with the forms of philosophical scepticism we have examined. It is assumed that all that is to count in the argument are the thoughts and experiences of people here and now, and that the only means of justification is the reasoning which we can do here and now. As with scepticism, which sees us as no more than subjects of sensory experience, utilitarianism and rights talk characteristically abstract from the full concrete reality of our experience.

I am not a pure bearer of rights. I do not simply receive pleasures and pains. Neither do I approach the world as pure reasoner, unburdened by a history, a past or a nature. As a moral being, deciding what to do and what to value, I am in fact as situated in my world as I am in my existence as a knowing agent.

To put this point in another way, my identity is a particular and specific amalgam of my biological nature and my social circumstances. And it is on the basis of what I inherit in these ways that I work out my conception of the good life, and what should count as reasons in evaluating which rights to recognize, which pleasures to seek, which pains to discount.

I am not a pure self. I am not self-sufficient, physically, psychologically, intellectually, emotionally or in any other way. I may be a rational animal, but I am an animal. I am also, in Alasdair MacIntyre's helpful phrase, a dependent rational animal. Multiple dependencies permeate my existence.

I owe to others my life, my language, my family, my locality, my nation, my culture, my education, my horizons and aspirations. Even if in these days of liberal individualism and autonomy, where I might have chosen my station in life and some of its duties, the station itself and many of its possibilities are given wholly or in part by factors outside my control or choosing.

I begin my life wholly dependent on others and on the possibilities they afford me. As I go through life, I gain a certain measure of autonomy, but I also establish other dependencies. Others may come to depend on me, but I also come to depend on them and on others. In old age I may revert to total dependency.

These multiple dependencies do not make me a puppet, but they do circumscribe my arena of choice. They substantially inform the terms in which I can think and act and plan. Even if I rebel in various ways, what I am rebelling against and hence the terms of my rebellion will be given to me by my society and my culture, and doubtless my temperament will play its part as well.

While not completely determining what I decide to do and think, the values I am brought up with and those of my surrounding society will form the context in which I judge those forms of behaviour that are acceptable, and those that are beyond the pale. So, to take an obvious example, we at the start of the third millennium might have a sense that the state should not interfere in private sexual acts performed by consenting adults. In this we might consider ourselves enlightened in contrast to those societies which used to punish homosexuality and outlaw adultery. On the other hand, some of those societies which were quick to condemn deviant sexual behaviour were far more liberal than us when it comes to acts of exchange and contract between freely consenting adults.

Similarly, we are far more sensitive to pain and suffering than many previous societies who were more prepared than us to tolerate both in order to achieve ends and types of character they believed important. Can you imagine a Childline in ancient Greece? Yet, had there been one, neither Marathon nor Salamis would have been won against the Persians, and there would never have been a fifth-century Athens or the philosophy of Socrates and Plato.

In pointing these things out, we need not prejudge who is right and who wrong on these or on other questions. But what we should conclude is that notions of right and of rights, and also of the acceptable limits of pleasure and pain, are far more complex and historically contingent than either rights theorists or utilitarians usually realize or imply.

We should also conclude that in practice, without the

background given to us by our existence in an actual, concrete society, talk of rights and the rest is largely empty and hopelessly underdetermined. It is in this sense that we should – in Edmund Burke's evocative phrase – regard society as a partnership between 'those who are living, those who are dead, and those who are to be born'.[11] We are formed as individuals in a particular society. It is from our society that we derive our identity and our selfhood. It is within our society that we derive our sense of obligation and of right. None of these things can exist in abstraction from the concrete circumstances in which they are realized.

As Burke himself put it, in commenting on the notion of the rights of man, if men dissolve their ancient corporation, in order to regenerate their community, in that state of things each man has a right, if he pleases, to remain an individual. In such circumstances, if anyone is then forced into the fellowship of another, this is conquest and not compact.

The point is that once we conceive of ourselves as fully independent individuals, without loyalty to an existing order, society will dissolve into an arena of permanent conflict. Each individual or group of individuals will have no resource but to assert their rights against the rest. Society will become ever more litigious, as each group becomes better able to use the machinery of the state. In the final analysis, in a situation of increasing alienation of individuals from their society, the state itself will come to seem, in Burke's phrase 'all-in-all', with the 'will, the want, the liberty, the toil, the blood of individuals . . . as nothing'. Something of this sort actually happened in the late and unlamented societies of the Eastern bloc in their final decades. As Vaclav Havel, among others, pointed out, during those decades no one from top to bottom actually believed the rhetoric which legitimated what was accordingly nothing but a demoralized tyranny, sustained by a combination of naked force and countless millions of petty and not-so-petty deceits. We still see today the effect in those countries of half a century or more of this systematic and enervating demoralization.

One of the most potent images of modern political thought is that of Thomas Hobbes' state of nature. Without society and without a ruler in Hobbes' view, human life is 'nasty, brutish and short', a 'war of all against all' in which the strongest flourish (for a time) and the weakest go to the wall. According to Hobbes, the solution is that individuals in the state of nature, realizing their predicament, agree by a 'social contract' to put themselves under a sovereign, who will keep the peace and enforce the rule of law.

Although while, in looking at various parts of the world today, we might recognize more than a grain of truth in Hobbes' vision of the state of nature, there are a number of problems with his solution. In the first place, how do we imagine that people outside any society could bind themselves or, more to the point, others, by a contract? If they could make a contract, they would already be social beings, and have no need of the primitive contract. But if they were completely outside any society they would have no reason to keep any pseudo-contract they might devise – except force. And, if the force of the state prevailed, isn't that just the situation envisaged by Burke, in which the war of all against all is replaced by the war of the state against all?

In view of the obvious difficulties with Hobbes' social contract, it is surprising to see a re-fashioned Hobbesianism dominant in contemporary philosophy. In John Rawls' highly influential *A Theory of Justice*[12] we are supposed to decide on the sort of social arrangements which would be ideal in a just society. In order to make this decision we have to think of ourselves as in the 'original position', a state of semi-ignorance in which we know general truths about human nature, but nothing about our own identity, our position in society, our abilities, or even our sex.

According to Rawls, choosers in this original position would opt for a society in which the state re-distributed basic goods and freedoms so that any inequalities would have to be seen to benefit the worst off (so, for example, doctors might be paid more than the average if this was the only way of ensuring that the least able and healthy got decent health care). It is hardly coincidental that this recipe is very much of a piece with the thinking of the dominant opinion-formers in the West today, who, like Rawls, want to square egalitarian feeling with the affluence made possible by inegalitarian enterprise.

But the detail of Rawls' own theory is not what is relevant here. What is relevant is his conception of society as a contract between anonymous and mutually unknown individuals. What, in such a society, could be the basis of loyalty or allegiance or even the sort of patriotism and affection which tie together all actually successful societies?

Where in such a society would be the 'pleasing illusions' and 'decent drapery of life' which, in Burke's terms, 'render power gentle and obedience liberal'?[13] Wouldn't the state be upheld purely by the force and ultimately the terror of its laws? In such a society the most rational thing for individuals and groups to do would be to capture the institutions of the state and divert them for their own purposes. The Hobbesian war of all against all would thus reproduce itself within the state, with the very institution which was supposed to defend us from the war being itself a major player in the battles. As already remarked, the regimes of the Soviet empire form one very pure illustration of this situation actually being realized. But we should not overlook the extent to which bureaucracies, even in Western democracies, are subject in their own way to capture by factional groups (often invoking the rhetoric of rights), and partly because of this, and partly because of their own unlovely methods, themselves contribute to alienation in a society.

However, despite all kinds of difficulties and deformations in all kinds of societies, the Hobbesian war of all against all remains a caricature of most actual human communities. In most actual communities people demonstrate all kinds of attachments of sentiment – to their families, to their friends, to their localities, to their clubs, to their schools and universities, to their roles and professions, to their countries and their institutions, to their religions, to the law itself and to much else besides. All this goes to make up the life of a people. Most of this life and most of the sentiment which underlies it is unchosen. Much is unreflected on.

It is far removed from the calculations of philosophers and political theorists. It is not founded in contract, and has little to do with the contracts of philosophers, though it constitutes the underlying fabric which makes such myths seem plausible. It is rarely touched on in the speeches of politicians, except when they lament its absence. But it forms the deeper bonding which ties a society together. It is what is presupposed by the more explicit thinking and policy-making which captures the public attention.

But there is a catch in attempting to restore this pre-political binding by political action. The reason for this is that too often the political direction and administration of people's lives mean that the state starts to do for them things they would be better doing for themselves. This erodes personal initiative and responsibility. People have the impression that the state will always step in to supply their needs, while at the same time they are prevented from doing many things for themselves (like arranging their health care or the education of their children). For those who come almost inevitably to rely on the state for the provision of basic needs, this initiates cycles of welfare dependency which can persist through generations.

Central to the pre-political bonding we are considering is a pre-reflective and unchosen sense of authority. In Hobbes' version, this authority came to be vested in the sovereign who emerged from the social contract. Hobbes realized, rightly enough, that a peaceable social life depended on a common acceptance of a final authority, a final court so to speak whose decisions and edicts would be regarded as binding on all.

But he and other social contract theorists misconstrue the actual situation of most of us. Most of us are born into a situation in which authority is already recognized, effectively sustaining and legitimating new contracts and policies. In talking of authority here, one is not referring to the authoritarian sovereign envisaged by Hobbes. What is being referred to is the sense by all in a society that there are moral rules and customs which are binding on all, and which circumscribe the limits of permissible action. This sense of authority would be required no less in a society whose political arrangements were egalitarian – as, arguably was the case in primitive hunter-gatherer societies and as, in a certain sense, is the case in modern democracies – as in societies arranged on hierarchical principles. Members of egalitarian societies still require a clear sense of how they should treat others and of how they can expect to be treated by others in their turn.

Even in circumstances of revolution, the revolutionaries characteristically appeal to a higher power than their own brute force and naked will. They appeal to the rights of man or divine justice or historical inevitability or a quasi-mystical 'will of the people' – supposedly transcending the factionalism of the actual people. Whether any of these claims are at all sensible, in making them they hope to gain for their actions the allegiance and loyalty which has deserted those they are overthrowing.

They will also, if they have any chance of success, be drawing on sentiments which are already powerful, if not always fully recognized, in their society. These include feelings about what is decent, what tolerable, what permissible; feelings which form the backdrop of the way of life of the people. It is this multiplicity of sentiment which makes social and political possible. Life together would be impossible did individuals not conceive themselves as living within all-pervading and pre-existing networks of duties, obligations, concerns and rights.

In many societies this sense of an authority binding on individuals and more basic than explicit political arrangements and decisions is given by religion. It seems likely that even the earliest human societies, now long lost in the mists of pre-history, had a religious sense. In almost all of the societies known to us before the modern era, religion and morality had been inextricably intertwined, each sustaining the other.

But this is no longer the case. We are now in the unprecedented situation of societies without any commitment on the part of their members to a religious basis to underpin their sense of right and wrong. And, as Nietzsche pointed out well over a century ago, this puts us into a profoundly problematic situation. We hope to have the – broadly – Christian ethic of compassion and respect for all, but without the Christian belief which makes these notions intelligible through seeing us all as children of God, and valued by Him. Can we continue to treat all human beings, however unprepossessing, as worthy of infinite respect in a society such as ours – materialistic, individualistic, hedonistic and technological? It may be possible, and only time will tell, but at the very least, we are sailing in uncharted waters.

Whatever turns out to be the answer to Nietzsche's question, and whether or not it is because there is still a residue of religious feeling even at the turn of the third millennium, the social and moral networks binding us together still by and large exist.

These networks are already there when particular individuals are born. It is from them that individuals derive their sense of identity. And they will continue after those living today are dead, in part to fulfil the hopes and expectations of those who went before.

All this is a large part of what is meant by thinking of

society as a contract between the living, the dead and the yet unborn. The living, of course, have their effect on the fabric of any society. All societies evolve; no society can be static. But equally, no society can start from scratch, or wipe away its past. Attempts to do so, even for the best of motives, are likely to erode the sentiment on which allegiance and a sense of mutual belonging rest. The state, rather than being that which protects those sentiments, enabling them to flourish, begins to seem an enemy. People begin to feel strangers in their own land.

It takes centuries to develop the traditions and institutions which bind a people together. It is because these things are the work of centuries that they often come to seem natural to those brought up to them. Of course they are not natural at all. Historians and sociologists are right to point out the often uncertain and unreliable way in which they have developed. But to the extent they have developed, they begin to define the way of life of a people. And then the cost of undermining them will be high, far higher than is envisaged by those who see politics only from the perspective of what seems reasonable to the present.

So, in abstract or in theory, it might seem good to set up a global order or a European super-state. That way there would be no more wars. Disputes between nations and peoples could be settled. Industry, commerce, welfare, defence, human rights and much else besides could all be organized efficiently and rationally. The claims of all and each could be fairly and openly adjudicated.

But who would do the adjudicating, and on what basis? How would the lives and claims of people with mutually conflicting loyalties and completely different traditions and institutions be synthesized? Only, it seems, by the central authority riding roughshod over local differences and sensibilities.

In the process local loyalties would be weakened, without any guarantee that supra-local loyalties could somehow replace them. In fact, if European experience is any guide, what would result would be hostility toward the central authority, which would be seen as serving no one's interests but those of the political and bureaucratic classes which ran it. The authority would come to be regarded as a piece of machinery worth capturing for furthering one's own ends. But it would not be respected as transcending sectional interests or seen as underpinning particular laws and policies (as, in different ways, both the American presidency and the British monarchy have come to be regarded).

None of this means that different nations and countries should not come together to agree on issues which concern us all, and which transcend national boundaries. Security and global warming would be two good examples of cases where little will be achieved without international negotiation. But there is no reason why negotiation on such trans-national issues should not be carried out in ways which respect local identities and traditions. There is no reason why all local differences have to be sunk into a global government or federation. There can (or could have been) a *Europe des Patries* (as de Gaulle hoped) as well as the kind of Europe envisaged by the Single European Act.

It is easy to see that any society which is more than a police state requires that those living in it should feel bound to it and in various ways obligated towards it and its institutions. What may be less easy for the generalizing philosophical mind to appreciate is that civil society emerges from a sense of a specific shared history and shared experience. These things are, of their nature, particular. Different histories and different experiences would produce different sets of expectations and different loyalties. While it is natural for human beings to lead some form of social existence, and to feel affection for their particular form of life, the forms themselves will be diverse and historically conditioned.

Some of these, unfortunately, will be objectionable. It is important to emphasize that recognizing that loyalty and sentiment are local and historically mediated does not mean that it is impossible to make judgements about their relative acceptability. We can make such judgements because we are reasoning beings and because we all share a common human nature. There are certain practices which would be inconsistent with human flourishing in any circumstances.

Slavery would be one example, and if there is anything right about the reflections of the last few pages, extreme individualism would be another. No doubt, too, we have learned through experience, if nothing else, that there is no reason why women cannot take on many of the roles formerly reserved for men, if not all of them.

Aristotle, notoriously, argued in favour of slavery and against women. But it could be pointed out that even at the time good reasons were available against him, on both scores. There was something unreasonable in Aristotle's view both then and now; or better, there is something unreasonable about his position at all times, when we consider timeless human nature, and what is required for its flourishing – at any time. No doubt in the future people will become more aware than most of us currently are of similar inconsistencies and irrationalities in our own thinking. But, as with us and with Aristotle, the argument will need to be against the background of what is needed at any time for human flourishing.

Saying this is not to deny that there are many different ways in which basic and universal human goods may be realized. Nor is it to underestimate the cost of undermining long-established tradition and sentiment. But it does suggest that a sensitivity to human history and diversity need not amount to a total relativism about human goods. It is possible to reason about these things, in a way which allows us to broaden and extend the perspectives we inherit.

For, as just remarked, beneath all the diversity and the conditioning there remains our biological nature. Reasoning about human flourishing must always take place within the broad general framework of our biological nature – as rational animals, to be sure, but animals with very specific natural constraints and needs. This brings us back to our original question about the constraints that human nature might impose on our development. The answer is that, just as we disregard history at our peril, it can be equally hazardous to ignore the facts of our nature.

In order to examine the meaning of this claim and its implications, I want now to look at two areas where we seem to have the power to transform our biological nature in radical ways. The first of these is in the area of genetic engineering, and the second concerns our attitude to sexuality.

To take genetic engineering first, we are now confronted

with the ability to engineer out of humanity all kinds of defects and illnesses. What this means in practice is that in the future people will not be born with genetic predispositions to conditions such as Down's syndrome, Huntington's chorea and possibly even heart disease, cancer and mental subnormality.

Foetuses with the offending genes will be identified at an early stage. They will either be aborted (as happens now in the case of Down's syndrome and spina bifida) or their genes will be modified so as to prevent the undesirable conditions developing. The research needed to produce these results will often involve experimentation on embryos, but (it will be said) we already produce surplus embryos in order to treat infertility.

There is also the very real possibility of cloning either animals or bits of myself and other humans in order to provide myself and others with spare organs when organs in living people break down or wear out. And research into cloning is also said to open the door to an existence in which the ageing process is held at bay for decades or even eliminated altogether.

Even from this brief survey it will be clear that we stand on the brink of as radical a transformation of our physical nature as could be imagined. And not only of our physical nature. Immense social and psychological changes will result if future populations are immune from disability and disease, if everyone is intelligent and (presumably) good looking, and if they live lives of eternal youthfulness.

Should we go down a road which promises such apparent benefits? If the only considerations are the utilitarian ones of the removal of pain and the promotion of pleasure, the answer would surely be that we should. Very likely the human rights view would tend in the same direction too. After all, doesn't everyone have a right to life, liberty and the pursuit of happiness? Many of the conditions which we might be escaping are ones which threaten life, impede people's freedoms and make the pursuit of happiness impossible.

And for many, an even more powerful argument in favour of pursuing genetic research and techniques will be real-life examples of suffering children and others whose conditions, it is said, could be alleviated were the research to be allowed to continue. Is an embryo of fourteen days really of such significance that it could not be used to save real human lives? Why shouldn't we clone animals or parts of ourselves in order to produce spare kidneys or livers, so people do not have to spend years on dialysis or face painful and untimely deaths?

Those who oppose genetic research and manipulation either here or elsewhere will often point to the potential dangers of such work. To take cloning, for example, thousands of pigs and hundreds of monkeys have been killed in the research, while those which have survived, and their offspring, are apparently liable to all sorts of abnormalities and deformities. It was hoped that stroke patients could be cured through injections of pig embryo cells, but all kinds of problems have arisen in the treatment. We have no idea of the long-term effects of introducing bits of animals into humans, nor can we tell in the long term what might happen were particular genes to be removed from the human gene pool. And there is the quite general point that any population needs a wide variety of genes to draw on; genes which seem quite useless at one time might turn out to be just what is needed in new circumstances. This flexibility could be lost were the genetic make-up of a species (in this case us) to be tightly controlled for specific purposes, particularly when the controllers (us) do not really know what we are doing.

All these points have some weight, and should make us very cautious. But they do not take us to the heart of the matter. The various practical difficulties may turn out to be exaggerated, or, by luck or very careful scientific work, it might be possible to avoid them. The real question is whether it is right even to attempt to revolutionize human nature, whether there might not be something fundamentally misguided, impious even, about the whole enterprise.

This would very likely be the conclusion drawn by those starting from a traditional religious position. Nature, including human nature, is part of God's creation. In assaulting nature, we assault God and His wisdom. Cloning and genetic manipulation do amount to an assault on the natural order of things. And insofar as our well-being depends on our keeping our place in the natural order of things, we very probably undermine our own chances of worldly satisfaction.

An argument of this sort would not command much respect among most contemporary philosophers. For them, nature is, as Darwin described it, not a piece of divine wisdom but the random and at times wasteful product of purely natural forces. If we can improve on nature, as we surely can, we certainly should.

Nevertheless, the intuition underlying the religious objection can be given a greater degree of support than might at first sight appear. To do this we need to consider how we might preserve a sense of the sacredness of human life, and then to consider more broadly the nature of our relationship to the natural world.

We have already seen in considering utilitarianism how we need to maintain a sense of the sacredness of each individual human life. Utilitarianism seemed faulty in that it trampled on this sense, treating individuals as exploitable for the greater good. Appeals to universal human rights require a belief that each and every one of us is, in some way, sacred, as does civilized life itself. The problem is to see how this vital sense of the sacredness of life can be maintained in the light of current and future medical developments. Certain barriers have been and are being crossed, to the detriment of us all, because once human life is regarded as disposable at one point, it will become very hard to hold the line at others, either logically or psychologically.

One such barrier concerns our attitude to potential human beings. In the space of 30 years in many Western democracies abortion has gone from being illegal or permitted only in the most stringent of circumstances to being available virtually on demand. Not to put too fine a point on it, abortion is now an extra form of contraception. The Pope is widely disliked for talking of a culture of death at the heart of Western society, but he has a point.

Leaving aside strictly religious considerations, the argument in favour of abortion is that foetuses do not have the mental or physical capacities of full human persons. This is undoubtedly true, but it is unclear how far this exonerates the deliberate destruction of a potential human being. After all, newly born babies and senile old people do not have the mental or physical capacities of full human persons. They may not even have the mental or physical capacities of some of the higher primates. Does it follow that they too may be killed in certain circumstances?

As things stand, the general public would probably be horrified by such a suggestion. But it is not difficult to find philosophers arguing in favour of the killing of severely handicapped babies and of the euthanasia of the severely senile on the grounds that the cases are not qualitatively different from the abortions most of us do tolerate. Given that the philosophers have logic on their side, and given too that these things undoubtedly occur in practice, how long will it be before there is general public acceptance of them?

Of course, the philosophers and doctors involved are not monsters. What they say is that certain lives are not worth living, and so would be better ended. But who is to say that a life is not worth living? Are the lives of those with Down's syndrome not worth living? (As it is, carriers of the syndrome are routinely aborted, which seems to be one main point of amniocentesis examinations.) Is it really, as one distinguished doctor said, a crime to bring a handicapped baby into the world? Or is it rather a crime to construct a world in which it is taken for granted that certain lives are less valuable than certain others, and in which certain lives will just not be allowed?

For this does seem to be the sort of world toward which medical science is moving us. We are in fact edging toward a world of eugenics, in which no one will be allowed to live who does not fulfil certain ideal specifications. At the moment only the very disabled are ruled out, but these things are relative. Today's below-average intelligence might be tomorrow's congenital idiot, regarded as a burden on him- or herself and on everybody else. Maybe in the not too distant future an unaesthetic appearance will be regarded as a severe disability. After all, if and when parents have the ability to alter the genes of their future children, won't it begin to seem the height of social irresponsibility to bring into the world someone who is more than usually stupid or ugly?

What we need to do before proceeding further down this road is to think carefully about just what the sacredness of life might mean. We might also think about dependence, about the fact that we are all dependent on each other in various ways. Is what we are saying that certain types of dependence are no longer to be tolerated? Do we take into account that while in obvious ways the disabled and the very old depend on us, in less obvious ways we depend on them. We depend on them for what they teach us about life and about ourselves, and also for providing us with a sense that there is more to life than is envisaged in the attitude which would judge their lives as having no quality at all.

Not that any of this means that we should not seek to alleviate disabling conditions. But not by any means. Maybe we have already gone too far in allowing experimentation on embryos. We are told that this is permitted only up to fourteen days after conception. But what will we say when some ingenious researcher tells us that if only he could experiment on a foetus of 28 days a cure for cancer would be within sight? Or on a recently aborted foetus? Or on a severely handicapped baby who will shortly die anyway?

Similar considerations apply to cloning. Once again we are told that the cloning of human beings will only be for therapeutic purposes, and even then involve only small collections of cellular tissue. But when it becomes possible to clone whole organs, so that I can have a new heart or kidney of my own without fear of rejection, the pressure will be very hard to resist. And if therapeutic cloning, why not cloning for reproductive purposes, or even for vanity? And what will such things do for generational continuity and for family structures, when one individual brings into being his own identical twin 50 years younger than himself? And who will be the new child's parents?

That similar conundra already arise in connection with some modern reproductive technologies simply shows that we may not have thought out the implications of what we are doing there either. For – apart perhaps from Plato – no one has so far given any detailed account of how social groups are to be organized which do not rely on a strong sense of family relationships and on the natural order of generations. What we do know is that in parts of the world where these things have broken down, there are considerable increases in social disorder and personal uncertainty. There is thus a strong indication that a social order which reflects the natural order in formally linking children to their natural parents has social and psychological advantages over more unnatural styles of arrangement.

In the last few paragraphs considerable use has been made of what are disparagingly called slippery slope arguments. A slippery slope argument assumes that any small concession or change in a particular direction is bound to lead to what are clearly unacceptable changes far down the same road; but, it is said, there is no reason why this should be so. Whatever might be said about slippery slope arguments in general, in the type of case we are considering, despite their critics, they do have a considerable plausibility.

Empirically there can be little doubt of this, as we saw in the case of abortion law reform, but similar points could be made about the dramatic way attitudes have changed over the last few decades on such matters as the acceptability of divorce and of illegitimacy. In all these cases the reason is plain to see. For once it is accepted that there is nothing essentially wrong with x in itself and that in certain circumstances x is permissible, it becomes very hard to draw the line at any point.

The same thing applies to the sacredness of human life. If human life is really sacred, then a line must be drawn around it, banning practices and procedures which conflict with its sacredness. To breach the line, even for the best of reasons, is tantamount to denying that we really hold that life is sacred. So every case and every new possibility can be argued for, and bit by bit, almost imperceptibly we get to the sort of situation I have been describing in which all kinds of human lives are regarded as dispensable. The worry is that in much of our current thinking on medical and genetic matters we are already on the wrong side of the line; with every 'advance', returning to the right side becomes that much more difficult.

If there is a strong argument for maintaining a sense of the sacredness of human life in general, what about particular aspects of the way we lead our lives? What about marriage, which is hardly a natural institution? What about our attitude to homosexuality where, it would be said, there has in recent years been a sea-change over what is acceptable or even 'natural'?

To take the second question first, there certainly is a tradition which found and continues to find homosexuality unnatural in a very specific sense. The point is not that homosexuality is not found in the non-human world, which may or may not be true, but which is hardly relevant to determining whether or not it is a bad thing for human beings to engage in. Nor is it that many people find homosexuality disgusting, which is true, but which is hardly enough to show that it is wrong. Nor does it amount to denying that some people may be born with an attraction to their own sex.

The point is rather about the natural purpose of the sexual act. The sexual act, it is said by thinkers in the Catholic-cum-Aristotelian tradition, has as its intrinsic purpose the procreation of children. That is what, in nature, it is aimed at. And that is what we human beings, in engaging in sexual activity, ought also to be aiming at. We should not use our sexuality deliberately to frustrate that natural purpose. If we do, we will do violence to the ultimate orientation of the act itself and – whether we admit it to ourselves or not – to our own underlying intention in performing it. So any form of sexual activity which deliberately makes procreation impossible is, in the strict sense of the word, a perversion. It perverts the natural end of the act and it perverts our own psychic health.

This traditional view is not stupid, and it has had some eminent defenders. Homosexuality would certainly count as wrong on that view. The only problem with it is that so would a great deal of heterosexual sexual activity, including any use of contraception. Masturbation too would be wrong. So if we are going to condemn homosexuality on grounds of unnaturalness, in consistency we would have to condemn a great many other practices which most opponents of homosexuality probably engage in themselves.

At the same time, debates about homosexuality, precisely because they are only about homosexuality, tend to obscure a sea-change in public attitudes to sex, of which acceptance of homosexuality is only one aspect. For we are managing to engineer a situation in which sexuality and procreation are largely separated both physically and psychologically.

On the one hand, we can freely engage in sexual activity, including 'normal' heterosexual activity, with the intention and in the certainty that there will be no children. In the past, and despite limited opportunities among some people for 'recreational' sex, for most people there was always the chance of pregnancy whatever precautions were taken. The link between sex and procreation was strong physically and emotionally. Much of the significance and meaning of the sexual act derived from that link.

On the other hand, we can now produce children without any normal sexual act. We have *in-vitro* fertilization and insemination by donors. We can store eggs and embryos to be hatched at convenience, without or long after any sexual congress. There is even the prospect of cloning, in which reproduction requires not even a vicarious donor.

With the links between sex and procreation becoming increasingly attenuated at both ends, so to speak, sex becomes more and more a recreational activity, for women as well as men. While sexual desire still engages strong feelings, it becomes questionable how long this will continue in a climate in which sex is treated and sold as a basically meaningless physical pleasure, with affection sometimes added. For those influenced by this climate it is indeed hard to discover anything wrong about homosexuality.

Should the separation between sex and procreation cause concern? It should for those who believe – as indeed empirical studies confirm – that a stable marriage between a heterosexual couple is the best environment for bringing up children. Sexuality still, for all the changes, engages some of our strongest feelings. Sex is an act which still is seen by most as having procreational possibilities, and even, as the old orthodoxy had it, a drive in that direction.

Many still see sexual love as having as its ultimate fruit the new life over which the love of the parents is then diffused, this transformed love being an essential ingredient in a normal upbringing. In both a physical and a moral sense, procreation through sexual love with one's spouse is the primary means by which the generations are linked and bonded.

Looked at in this way, and despite all kinds of institutional variations and deviations over history, traditional monogamy can be seen as a way in which culture builds on natural facts. These facts include the basic facts of conception and birth, the long time human children need care and nurture, and the dynamics of male and female desire. Marriage thus builds with the grain of nature, to the benefit of all parties: for the children, as it provides them with a stable environment in which to develop; for the wife, whose links to her husband are secured and sanctified; and for the husband, whose existence is given meaning and consolation through the responsibilities and ties he takes on.

There is, then, a strong argument for any society which has it continuing to give the traditional institution of monogamous marriage a privileged place, even as it tolerates other forms of sexual activity. If there is a movement away from this at the start of the twenty-first century, it can be seen as part of a wider drift away from the natural order of things, which is made possible by science and technology. Many are worried by this trend, and rightly so.

This is not just because of the potential disasters which may come from this trend. Even if all the new technologies and possibilities turned out to be perfectly safe, there would still be cause for concern at the way our fundamental orientation towards nature is being altered. At root we are, and remain, products of the natural order. To put it at its most basic, our health and sanity depend on our maintaining that order and our links with it.

It is not simply that we owe nature a debt for our existence. It is rather, as we know from experience, and has been eloquently described by E. O. Wilson in *Biophilia*,[14] that a life lived in a wholly artificial technological environment is one against which our deepest instincts rebel. Whether this leads in a religious direction or not, this widely remarked fact tells us that we are part of a natural process on which our flourishing depends. In assaulting nature and in severing our bonds with it, we assault ourselves.

This is not to say that nature should not be worked on by us, and transformed in various ways. After all, the countryside which, despite industrial-scale farming and new towns, we all cherish, is the fruit of centuries of human effort and transformation. And so are cities like Venice, ancient Athens, Siena and St Petersburg. But what we need to cultivate is a sense in which our work goes with the grain of nature, rather than obliterating nature's forms and processes, and which respects natural materials and divisions, as opposed to obliterating nature's every trace.

Thus, we might point to the way in which Venetian architecture is largely constructed from local stone, and in which its forms and colours reflect natural forms and colours, contrasting that with the geometric forms, concrete, glass and artificial lighting and heating characteristic of modern architecture. We might contrast gardening and organic farming, which build on and develop tendencies already in nature, with cloning and xenotransplantation, which definitely do not. The one subverts the natural process by which life is transmitted. The other strikes at the concept of a species, something which has evolved naturally over countless generations.

I am not here claiming to be providing conclusive arguments for particular conclusions about nature's grain. Nor, to pick up on our earlier discussions, am I showing exactly when we are transgressing the boundaries which mark where the sacredness of human life begins, and which must not be transgressed. This is not the place for the detailed examination of cases which would be required.

But what I am claiming is that in our consideration of these matters we need to take into account factors which in contemporary utilitarian and right-based thinking are overlooked. We need, as Roger Scruton has urged,[15] to recapture a notion of piety – towards nature, towards individual human beings, however weak or unattractive, and towards the history and institutions of our community.

Many contemporary ills and difficulties arise because we are no longer pious – to nature, to others or to the fabric of our social existence.

Piety derives from the ancient Roman virtue of *pietas*, that is, respect for parents and ancestors, for the gods of the household, for law and the civil order, and for appointed festivals and public ceremonies. In Roman times these things were honoured out of a sense of gratitude for things which were not chosen but inherited, and which formed the framework of civilized life.

Of course in Roman times there was also the very real contrast with life in other societies which did not know *pietas*; in Roman society itself, particularly in the Empire, it was always possible to see what happened in one's own society when *pietas* was forgotten. In contemporary Western society, piety is not so much forgotten as never explicitly acknowledged in the first place.

Yet there is growing disquiet at the various ways in which we seem to be developing where we are losing touch with our roots, natural and historical. In an obscure way, many do recognize our frailty and dependence, even though public discourse gives little scope for that recognition, which means that the disquiet often expresses itself in crude and irrational ways.

We emphasize our individuality, to be sure, but we also know that much is required to create and to sustain that individual selfhood. What is required to sustain it is both natural and cultural. We know that unprecedented changes are being made in both areas, and this makes us uneasy, for all the immediate benefits these changes appear to bring us.

In many of the changes we evince no reverence for the

conditions which sustain us and which have produced us. We seek to deny the fragility of our existence and its ultimate mystery. And in these failures we are in danger of undermining the very things which make our all too fragile lives humane and tolerable.

6 **Science**

Science is one form of rational inquiry about the world. It is rightly highly influential. Particularly since the sixteenth century, natural science has led to astonishing increases in our knowledge of the physical world. These increases go from knowledge of the very small, in quantum theory where quantities can be accurately calculated to twenty decimal places, to the very large, in astro-physics. We have comprehensive theories of electricity and magnetism, of gravity, and of space and time. We now have fairly complete accounts of chemical substances and elements, and their relationships to the smaller particles which compose them. In biology we now understand the mechanisms of life itself (even if not how it actually came about).

Alongside all this accretion of theoretical knowledge and, to an extent depending on it, there have been corresponding developments in technology, particularly over the last 200 years. The world in which we live has been transformed out of all recognition, and so have the comforts and devices available to all, at least in the developed world.

All these facts are so obvious they hardly need stating. There are, of course, criticisms of the environmental effects of the applications of science. Some of these criticisms should certainly be taken seriously, particularly those which might suggest a lack of piety on the part of the human race. But that does not impugn the knowledge which makes impiety possible. Rather it validates it as knowledge, because if our technologies were not based on truth, they would not work at all, even to despoil nature and undermine the respect we should have for the natural order.

It is also true that some of our scientific ideas have difficulties of a theoretical nature. As has often been pointed out, quantum theory is full of difficulties and so-called paradoxes which appear insoluble so long as we remain within its framework. (And, for dealing with the very small, we have no other framework even in prospect, which is itself a testament to the very successes of the framework we do have in predicting very precisely what will happen in any set-up.)

Neither is it at all clear how quantum theory and relativity might be brought into one comprehensive account of the physical world. It looks as if what we have at the level of fundamental physics are partial and partly unsatisfactory accounts of bits of that world, whose mutual relationships are not well understood.

There is also what philosophers of science like to call 'the pessimistic meta-induction'; that is, in the history of science even the most successful of past theories (such as Newton's, for example) have eventually been rejected on the basis of new theories, new evidence. So why should this not eventually prove true of our favoured theories, especially given the well-known difficulties of some of them?

To which the answer is presumably that there is no reason at all as to why our currently held theories should not in the future be replaced by better theories. But saying that is not to say that quantum theory, let us say, does not contain a great many truths, just as Newton's theory did. And in any transition to a successor theory, those truths will have to be retained. As these truths include, among other things, the information which allows us to split atoms, produce nuclear power, zap cancer cells and much else besides, it is obvious that an awful lot of existing knowledge will have to be taken into any new theory and explained by it. We may re-configure our understanding of what sub-atomic particles and forces are, but what will not be re-configured will be our knowledge of the things which are done by these particles and forces, and the circumstances in which they are done.

There are, then, difficulties and uncertainties about scientific knowledge, but they are not such as to impugn the whole edifice, or to impugn the belief that there have been great advances in that knowledge. As with other forms of scepticism, scepticism about scientific progress cannot be entirely ruled out. It is just possible that the advances which have been made, including all the specific discoveries from planets to particles, from genes to gamma rays, could all be mistaken. It is just possible that in all this, humanity could be the victim of some cruel cosmic deception, in which things consistently, predictably and regularly seem to us to be thus and so, and yet are really (in some obscure sense of 'really') quite different.

Yet even as we entertain such scepticism, we should ask ourselves this. Compared to the daily experience and refined experimentation and observation which gives us grounds for our scientific beliefs, what evidence do we have for any cosmic deception hypothesis? Within science we may have grounds for specific worries, where predictions do not come out as they are supposed to. We may also wonder whether, in quantum theory and relativity, say, we might not be at the very boundary of what is actually intelligible for minds such as ours. But these are doubts for which there are specific reasons, and about areas which, in contrast to other parts of science, remain unclear and problematic. To repeat, unclarity at the level of over-arching pictures of an area of science does nothing to impugn the data which those pictures are invoked to explain. It is this vast mass of data about the world which it makes little sense to doubt, and which in recent centuries has grown so remarkably.

Nevertheless, having said all this and having rejected any general scepticism about the truth of science, we still need to come to terms with just what it is that science is teaching us. In particular we need to examine the relationship between scientific accounts of the world and what we experience in our day-to-day lives. For science presents us with accounts of the world in general and of human life in particular which seem to wipe out much of what is significant to us.

To see how this might be, we can go back to the beginning of modern science, to Galileo himself. Galileo said that it was his intention to investigate the phenomena of the physical world in terms of their shape, size, position and quantity of motion; in other words, in terms of their measurable features. Qualities such as colour, sound, smell, taste and feel, which seemed notoriously subjective and unstable anyway, would not enter the explanations offered by the new physics.

This scientific relegation of what came to be referred to as 'secondary' qualities became further entrenched under Newton. Newton argued in his *Opticks* that colour did not exist in the real world. In the real world particles were colourless. Our impression that the world consisted of coloured objects was due to colourless particles hitting our retinas and setting up a chain of activity in our brains which gave us the experience of colour. And similar accounts were to be given of the perception of sound and the other secondary qualities.

The conclusion was inevitably drawn from all this that secondary qualities were merely subjective, artefacts of human experience, in contrast to the objective, primary qualities of shape, size, position, velocity and so on.

So the scientific picture of the world seemed to remove from it some of its central features, humanly speaking. And scientific disenchantment continued apace. In the eighteenth century, for all Newton's own mysticism, once the Newtonian vision became established, God became redundant. At best God was the remote architect of the universe and its laws. But once the system had been set up, God played no part in things. For explaining what actually happens in the world, there was no need to invoke God: things just happened as scientific laws said they had to.

Nor, increasingly was there any room for human spirits or souls or even free will. After all, we are part of the physical world. We are subject to its laws, just as much as atoms and billiard balls. It should be possible to give scientific accounts of human behaviour which use only the concepts and explanations of science. Even if we talk of ourselves as being motivated by our desires, guided by our beliefs and making our own choices, all this is ultimately dispensable. We are just bits of matter, who seem to ourselves, for convenience, to be desiring, believing and choosing. But in the final analysis, a full account of our actions could be given in terms of the activity of the particles which make up our limbs and organs and of the electro-chemical processes of our brains and nervous systems. We do not need to appeal to desires, intentions or conscious states, talk of which is notoriously vague and hard to pin down and quantify, in contrast to the hard, measurable and objective primary qualities, with which science deals.

There are a number of things going on in all this. First, in the elimination of secondary qualities there is a desire to explain phenomena in the most basic and general ways. Perhaps we can account for the processes which produce in us the perception of colour without mentioning colour itself. Were such an explanation possible, it would be a very model of explanation. It would be showing how something came about without mentioning that thing. It would be explaining it as the effect of more basic things.

Of course, insofar as science is simply explaining our perception of colours and other secondary qualities, it assumes that they exist, that they are real and that they are more or less as we perceive them. There would otherwise be nothing to explain. But many who take the scientific path go one step further. They conclude that because there are no colours or secondary qualities in the account which explains our perception of them, there are no colours or secondary qualities in the world. Colours and secondary qualities are then construed as illusions produced in us and due simply to the activity of our brains.

They are then 'explained' in the same way that someone who does not believe in ghosts explains ghosts; that is to say, he explains how it is that people come to have the illusion that there are ghosts. But the sceptic about ghosts already has reasons (or prejudices) against the reality of ghosts. That is his starting point. In the case of the scientific explanation of colour, by contrast, we do not start with any assumption that there are no such things. Neither is this conclusion forced on us by the scientific account, any more than we would be forced to conclude that there are no living things, just because living processes can be seen as arising from non-living matter. Indeed, for all that has so far been shown, secondary qualities and living things could both be examples of realities which emerge from more basic levels of existence.

However, over and above any conclusions about their real existence, in the elimination of secondary qualities from the scientific picture of the world, there is a second line of thought. It is that in its accounts and explanations, science ought to use the most general concepts possible. Described sometimes as 'an absolute point of view' or even as 'the view from nowhere', the aim is that a scientific explanation should be intelligible to any intelligence, whatever its particular sensory constitution. Thus, it may be that the perception of colour is possible only for creatures with eyes like ours. Vision itself requires eyes, and there could be rational beings without eyes. So, ideally, scientific explanations should not make use of properties accessible only to creatures with eyes or with colour vision.

None of this would in itself show that there are no such things as colours. It would simply indicate that colour is the sort of thing which only certain beings can perceive. But, following on from this, there is a not unreasonable assumption that the less relative a particular type of explanation is to creatures of particular sensory make-ups, the more likely that explanation is to capture the most basic features of the world.

Finally, there is in science, and as part of science, the attempt to analyse our own activity from outside, as it were, as part of science's domain. So we see ourselves as elements in the physical universe, as subject to its laws and forms of causality. Again, a form of objectivism is at work, linking with the denial of secondary qualities and the impulse to a highly general form of explanation. It is the thought that in a complete explanation of things, including human things, subjective experiences and feelings and thoughts will play no part.

The vision of the world which emerges from these tendencies has been described as disenchanted; but it is far more than that. 'Dehumanized' would be a better description, for it is a world with no secondary qualities, and in which human beings themselves were just complexes of particles, acting as particles act. There would be no human landmarks in this world, for there would be nothing but particles and forces. There would be no guarantee that the particular configurations picked out in this scientific vision would correspond to the everyday objects of the world of human experience, and even if they did they would not be seen in terms of our needs and interests.

In one sense there need be no objection to this scientific account. If an account which abstracts systematically from everything of human interest or concern is the most economical way of doing physics, well and good. After all, physics is not about human interests and concerns: it is about forces and the behaviour of particles; it is about the way objects are composed of elementary particles and governed by fundamental forces. Success in this enterprise, far from needing inclusion of the humanly relevant in its accounts, requires its elimination.

The problem, if there is one, is not with physics or science. It is not even with the terms and concepts which a particular science includes or excludes. Problems are going to arise only when a science, such as physics or biology, implies that its concepts and explanations capture the whole of the reality.

So, inspired by Newtonian accounts of colour, many philosophers and scientists have claimed that really there is no such thing as colour. And there are philosophers today who are described as eliminative materialists. In accordance with the reductionist line of thought described earlier, they believe that in principle it would be possible to offer a complete account of human behaviour which made no reference to anything mental, such as thoughts or desires. Scientifically speaking, we should confine ourselves to describing neural activity and physiological processes. In everyday life we would no doubt continue to speak about people as having mental states and processes, and these states and processes as having something to do with how they behave, but mental talk is, in principle eliminable; in a scientifically cleansed account of the world it would be, and there would in such an account be nothing essential left out.

We are here at the hard theoretical edge of things. But even for those happy to allow that colours really exist and that there is something ineliminably mental about us, there is often a sense that what we can learn from science is somehow more true, more objective than anything else. This attitude is particularly significant when it comes to questions of public policy. Only the scientifically measurable is truly objective, and should be allowed to determine policy decisions.

We may call the attitude that only the scientifically determinable is true or objective or important 'scientism'. Scientism is not itself forced on us by science. The prestige of science and its success may incline us toward scientism, but there is no necessary move from science to scientism. One can admire science and its achievements without holding that science can tell us everything worth knowing. One can be a scientist without believing that science can explain everything, or that only 'scientific' considerations should influence policy.

Conversely, one can know little about science and yet be, in various respects, scientistic. One can, in common with many philosophers, believe that in principle science can explain everything. (That scientism of this sort might be a commoner condition than one might suppose would itself be a testament to the power and influence of science, even among some who might think of themselves as critical of science.)

Let us now examine some of these claims. First, there is the view that only those things which science admits as fundamental are really real. To see what this claim might actually do to our picture of the world, consider the following passage from Proust:

> The town that I saw before me had ceased to be Venice. Its personality, its name, seemed to be lying fictions which I no longer had the courage to impress upon its stones. I saw the palaces reduced to their constituent parts, lifeless heaps of marble with nothing to choose between them, and the water as a combination of hydrogen and oxygen, external, blind, anterior and exterior to Venice, unconscious of Doges or of Turner.[16]

Proust was writing of a sense of depression which had come over him after he had been cruel to his mother, but the passage illustrates admirably what would be lost humanly speaking in a strictly scientific description of the world.

Within a scientific account, there can be no objection to such a description. But it does not follow that a description replete with humanly charged meanings is thereby a collection of lying fictions. The name 'Venice' presupposes bits of human history. Venice is composed of stone and rises from the sea, but it is not just a physical object. It is an institution whose significance could be understood only given an acquaintance with human beings, their history and their ways. But what Venice is and what it means do not somehow become subjective just because creatures from some other part of the universe might not grasp these things.

No more do colour or sound become unreal just because their perception requires sensory organs of a particular sort, any more than radio waves become unreal just because they are imperceptible without radio receivers. For creatures with the right equipment (us, for example) colours, sounds and the rest of the secondary qualities have all the requisites of objective properties. We can distinguish between a thing's real colour and its merely apparent colour. We can agree on what its colour is. Its colour is normally something which has enough stability to make judgements about its 'true' colour checkable. What more might be wanted for objectivity, unless one has already made a dogmatic decision that only the scientifically fundamental will count as real?

It might be said that colour and the other secondary qualities are not causally fundamental. They themselves are produced by wavelengths of light and sound of specific frequencies and other physical factors which can be fully described without reference to secondary qualities. Once again, though, this does not show that colour and other secondary qualities do not exist. And even if colour and the rest may not feature in a scientific account of causes, this does not mean that they do not have causal effects.

They certainly do in the human world, where much of what we do is affected by our perceptions of secondary qualities. And whatever might be true in a scientific analysis of colour, in terms of wavelengths and so on, my decision to paint my door just the shade of blue that I choose is motivated by the way the colour appears to me – and to others – in relation to the rest of the colours in my room. In other words, crucial to an explanation of my choice of the paint and of others' reaction to it will be its nature as a secondary quality, having the appearance it does to suitably constituted observers.

So there is no need for any general rejection of the reality or objectivity of secondary qualities. There is no need to think that they are not a genuine part of the world, or that we somehow paint them onto an otherwise colourless, soundless, textureless, tasteless and odourless world.

No more is there any need to accede to the other part of the scientistic picture, that reference to human thoughts, feelings, beliefs, emotions and experiences is somehow dispensable in an account of our behaviour.

The first point to make here is that an account of human behaviour which omitted those things would not be an account of human behaviour – it would be an account of our physical movements which left out just those aspects which make them into something more than the reflex activity of nervous systems. It would leave out the way in which a physically similar movement of my arm was, on one occasion a gesture of affection, on another a threat, and on yet another a signal of my intention to turn right.

It would also leave out all that goes to make this bundle of limbs and organs in front of me the child I love, or my rival at work, or my drinking companion. For when we react to each other as persons, we are reacting to them as beings with motives, intentions, desires, emotions, beliefs, characters, and so on; in other words, as manifesting just those attributes and attitudes which eliminative materialism says are dispensable. Could science show that they are indeed dispensable? It is hard to see how it could.

In the first place, science itself is a human activity. The way we present it disguises this fact, and disguises the way science grows out of human life and human aspirations. Scientific findings are typically expressed in an impersonal way, but this cannot entirely disguise the way in which they are accepted because human beings think that they are true – and also interesting to human beings, a point to which we shall return.

In considering the nature of science as an activity, we are

taken back to our earlier consideration of Socrates in *Phaedo.* For human beings engage in what it seems to them good to engage in. So science exists because we, or some of us, find it good to engage in it.

Moreover, in doing it, we, or those who do it, make judgements all the time about what is true, probable, supported by evidence and, once more, interesting. In making these judgements we presuppose that the structures of human intentionality are not wholly illusory. We presuppose that we do in fact make judgements, have ambitions, try to find out what is true or useful, or whatever; and that some at least of what emerges actually is true, useful, fulfils our scientific and other ambitions, and so on.

So, can an activity show that there is something amiss with the conditions which actually make it possible? Could science demonstrate that our conception of ourselves as enquirers should actually be eliminated in favour of some other story about bones and sinews, and nerves reacting and neurons firing, and so on, which made no reference at all to our intentions in doing the activity or to the validity of our beliefs and judgements?

Considered in general terms, science does not necessarily undermine our conceptions of ourselves as free and rational agents. It is quite legitimate for branches of science like physics or chemistry to focus only on particular aspects of reality. Without such simplifications, it is hard to see how science could proceed at all, and there is clearly a point in seeing just how much can be explained from one specific point of view. So in concentrating just on what physics or chemistry deal with, one need not be denying that there are other aspects of things which cannot be fully dealt with by the laws of physics or the equations of chemistry.

Life might be such a phenomenon. Physical scientists are not, *qua* physical scientists, committed to holding that biology can be reduced to physics and chemistry. It remains an open question. Maybe there are processes in the biological realm which cannot be explained in physical or chemical terms, and which need their own special level of explanation. Perhaps the impulse to survive and reproduce and the workings of the evolutionary process are not foreshadowed in the inorganic realms of physics and chemistry. Neither is it easy to see just how all the physico-chemical conditions needed to produce even a primitive living cell come about just by chance. So many of them need to be in place and in the right place all at once to make their chance creation through a strike of lightning in the primeval soup almost wholly incredible.

Even more than life itself, consciousness looks hard to explain in terms of inorganic processes. Just how can physical processes in the brain produce thought and sensation? How can a material object, such as an animal or human being, become a centre of awareness? How can all the diverse impulses which we receive from the world via our several sensory organs combine in our brain or mind to produce a single, united stream of experience?

Evolutionary biology and psychology can give partial accounts of particular mental functions, even linking them up in some cases with particular bits of the brain. Thus, pain is to promote the avoidance of danger, and is associated neurologically with stimulation of the c-fibres. The development of human intelligence, associated particularly with the neo-cortex, is (in the latest account) to do with our ability to compete with our fellow humans in the quest for mates.

But these explanations, such as they are, assume that we do have consciousness, thought and experience, and deal with particular applications of them. What they do not explain, and what we have hardly any handle on at all, is how consciousness, thought and experience can be produced by material processes at all. The most we can do is to correlate these mental phenomena with brain activity. But however fine-grained these accounts get, they do nothing to solve the basic enigma, which is how mental states and experience can emerge from physical matter, nor at a physical level are the mental events ever perceived. All that can be perceived are the firings of neurones and other electro-chemical activity, a point anticipated long ago by Leibniz who pointed out that if the brain were big enough to walk through, thought and experience would still never be observed.

Faced with these and other difficulties, it may be reasonable to conclude that life and consciousness may need special circumstances in which to emerge. They will also need special sciences to deal with them. This will be biology in the case of living processes and organism. As for a science of consciousness, beyond being able to correlate some brain processes with some types of conscious state, at present we remain almost entirely in the dark. We just do not know what form an explanation of how material processes produce experience might take.

In saying that special sciences beyond physics and chemistry are needed to explain certain things, one would be implying that physics and chemistry are not complete.

That is, one would be saying that there are things which those sciences, even taken together, cannot explain.

But it is not part of physics or of chemistry to declare themselves complete in this sense. All that they say are that all processes described in physical and chemical terms will be subject to the laws of physics and chemistry. It is another claim altogether, a philosophical claim, that all processes in the universe can be described in physical and chemical terms without leaving out anything vital to their existence or behaviour.

On the other hand, the philosophical claim is very tempting. If everything cannot be fully described and explained in terms of physics – the most fundamental and general of the sciences – where do these extra bits come from? Do they emerge mysteriously, as it were, from nowhere? Or is all matter potentially living and potentially conscious from the start – in which case physics could be seen as the science which deals with matter insofar as those potentials are not manifested.

Thoughts of any kind of emergence or of potentialities which, throughout the universe are mostly never manifested, make many people uncomfortable. They sound mystical as well as mysterious, with echoes of the now largely discredited vitalism of the early twentieth century. And in truth, for all that physics and chemistry do not declare themselves complete, science does pose us with a dilemma when it comes to human behaviour. This dilemma would not disappear even if we admitted that biology and a science of consciousness required conceptual and explanatory resources beyond those of the sciences of inorganic matter.

The dilemma arises from the very attempt to give a scientific account of human behaviour, of whatever sort. Baron d'Holbach, a noted philosopher of the European Enlightenment, was lavish in his praise of science. He declared that if only mankind could, through science, free itself from ignorance, we would find ourselves on the verge of an era of unprecedented prosperity and peace. Inspiring as Holbach's dream may have been at the time – and visions of this sort did inspire many at the end of the eighteenth century – it is misleading on at least two counts.

In the first place, it is simply not the case that scientific knowledge, as such, leads to material improvements. Holbach himself should have known this. He wrote 200 or more years after Copernicus, 150 after Galileo and a century after Newton. Yet at the time there had been very few material improvements as a result of science. The industrial revolution was only just beginning at the start of the nineteenth century, and had far more to do with the harnessing of steam power, the automation of spinning and the production of iron than with knowledge of the laws of Newton.

More significant, though, than uncertainties over the practical effects of scientific knowledge, is the way that knowledge tends to impact on human life and culture. It is obvious that scientific advances, such as those of Copernicus, Galileo, Newton and Darwin have disenchanted the universe. That is, following these discoveries, it is no longer possible to see the world as full of gods and divine interventions. For reasons we will explore more fully in Chapter 8, it is no longer as easy as once it was to see the world as the handiwork of a divine designer or controlled by a benevolent Providence.

This should not be seen as pure loss. Or rather, if it is loss, it is loss of illusion, however painful and difficult losing such illusions may be (something thinkers like Holbach tend to underestimate). Hard or not, though, if we are seekers after truth or wisdom, we can hardly complain at learning that some cherished and pious beliefs are just incompatible with the way the world is.

But where the impact of science is far more questionable is in its effects on our own self-image, for here we seem to be caught between two conflicting and incompatible perspectives, a conflict bound to arise when we regard ourselves as objects for scientific investigation, rather than the subjects performing those investigations.

In seeing myself as an object for scientific investigation, I take a stance outside myself. I will see myself as an object caused to act as it does by all sorts of forces. These forces will include things both inside and outside me. They will include the effects of my environment and upbringing, as well as the stimuli I receive from moment to moment. They will also include my motives, emotions, beliefs and feelings; but insofar as these can be scientifically explained, they will be seen as due to other, earlier causes, such as my genetic make-up, my precise character and, once again, my environment. None of these earlier causes are caused by me, and none of them do I control. I have been formed by them and continue to be controlled by them.

So where in this story do I come in? Where are the choices and feelings I am actually responsible for, and which I am not simply pushed and pulled by forces outside my control to adopt?

According to the influential accounts of human

behaviour which followed on the scientific enlightenment, really such things are nowhere. The psychology of the Enlightenment itself was that we human beings operated under the dictates of the twin masters of pleasure and pain. For all our high-sounding talk of reason and freedom, all we are really doing in any of our actions is to avoid pain and promote pleasure, in however disguised a way. And this is what we are programmed by nature to do.

This psychology is given a socio-economic twist by Marx. Our failure to understand our true motives on an individual level is compounded by our failure to understand the way our culture and social institutions are driven by economic forces and serve the interests of the rulers. We are systematically deceived about our institutions, our legal system and our culture more generally. All these things are as they are because they serve the interests of the stronger. We ascribe universal validity to our institutions and beliefs, but this is because we do not really understand their restricted extent or the way in which they have actually come to dominate our lives (a view still held by the deconstructionist descendants of Marx). There are endless disputes among the followers of Marx about the extent to which he thought that conscious human activity could liberate men from their servitude to economic forces, but there is no doubt that he believed that for most of history and for most of humanity, men were unwitting victims of social and economic forces. They were unwitting particularly in the way they take local beliefs and practices, which actually simply served the interests of those in power at the time, as being in some sense freely held and universally valid.

Freud gives a further elaboration of enlightenment

psychology. According to him, our surface consciousness is simply a mask for darker sexual forces which are really running the show, and which, through repression, we hide and distort. As with Marx, but in a different way, our understanding of our motivation is systematically deceived. We are largely at the mercy of forces we neither understand nor recognize (until enlightened by Marx or Freud, as the case may be).

And Darwin, once again highly fashionable, would have us at the mercy of a relentless and ruthless drive to survive and reproduce. In the latest interpretation of Darwinian theory, what largely impels what we do is not our conscious thought at all. It is unconscious genes, which use and colonize human beings and other complete organisms in order to serve their drive to replicate themselves. In this case, we are unwitting prisoners of our genes, just as, in the other two cases, we are prisoners of the forces of production and of our unconscious respectively.

All these views continue to influence us in countless ways. But the detail of the different explanations is perhaps less significant than their shared and overall form. For each of them would have it that we are subject to forces we do not understand or recognize (prior to being enlightened, of course). Each has it that in our conscious thinking about our motives and our choices we are systematically deceived.

We might think that we are pursuing justice by entering parliamentary politics, but we are really serving the interests of the capitalist state. We might think that we are studying hard at school out of a desire to enter a privileged community of scholars, but really we are trying to displace our father in the affections of our mother. We may think that we are acting in a generous or altruistic way simply because that is the good thing to do. But actually, we are just playing a game of evolutionary tit-for-tat. What we are really doing in being kind, say, is attempting to ensure that others help us at some time in the future when we need help ourselves, so that we may eventually get into an advantageous position enabling the genes within us or our children to replicate themselves.

Given that on all these accounts what we think we are doing is not what we are actually doing or what is actually causing what we do, it is not surprising that scientific accounts of our behaviour tend toward eliminative materialism. That is, they tend toward the view that in a fully scientific account of human behaviour we can and should dispense with reference to conscious thoughts and beliefs altogether. For what goes on in us at the conscious level falsifies the true springs of our activity. On this view the work being done by our conscious thoughts and intentions becomes a mere show, an illusion covering up the reality. So it is not surprising to find those who hold this view questioning whether we should not simply discount what is on the conscious surface of our lives. Our mental life becomes a wheel which turns nothing.

But this belief is itself unlivable. We cannot act as if we are not conscious choosers, and as if most of our beliefs and decisions are not what they seem. We can, of course, admit that sometimes we are self-deceived. In both belief or choice what we think we are doing is sometimes a cover for some less reputable thought or intention. Not all the institutions of our society are exactly what they seem. There is that much truth in Marx and Freud and even Darwin, and there is room in our lives and societies for a degree of unmasking. But the case that needs to be unmasked cannot be the normal case. It is precisely in contrast to the normal case that we pick out the cases where things are not as they seem.

Neither is this a purely 'first person' point. It is not just about my experience. In dealing with others, we do not – normally – treat them as driven beings, passive victims of delusions or forces over which they have no control. Again, while this may sometimes be the case, it will be in contrast to the normal case where people mean what they say, and their apparent motives are their real ones.

Our dealings with others depend on our reacting to them as if they are the instigators of their actions, and that, on the whole, they know what they are doing and saying, and that they have reasons for what they say and do. We may criticize those reasons or regret what they do, but we think of others as normally transparent to themselves. And in treating them in this way, we usually find our expectations fulfilled. Social life goes on well enough on that basis. By contrast there would be no social life if we discounted the reasons people have for what they do and their normal understanding of their institutions, for we would not be treating each other as persons, but rather as objects in some causal process over which we and they have no real insight or control.

Others are not normally the unwitting victims of forces they neither understand nor control. And if they are victims of manipulation in this sense, it is a matter for political reform or personal therapy. It is something to be put right. But there can be a putting right in this area. The situation in which people are deceived or self-deceived can be replaced by a better situation in which they are enabled to act as they think they are acting, and for the reasons they think they have.

It is not, as in the eliminative account, that reasons are done away with altogether in favour of non-rational and unconscious brain processes. Nor is it, as in the Darwinian or Freudian or Marxist accounts, that there is only one possible set of motives to drive us, and a rather disreputable set at that.

So, in attempting to treat ourselves as objects for scientific investigation, we are led to falsify our most basic experience of ourselves and of other people as agents who are conscious and free and rational. We may take this stance for a time, just as a surgeon may look at the organism beneath his knife as a kind of ill-functioning machine rather than as a person, a friend, a lover, a parent, a writer, a teacher, a chemist, or whatever.

But adopting the scientific perspective on ourselves or on others is possible only during those periods in which we consciously and intentionally push our normal attitudes to persons to one side. In other words, it is when we cease to regard others or ourselves as persons. It is as much a falsification of our basic orientation to the world as is the philosophical scepticism we examined earlier.

None of this means that we have to abandon science, even scientific inquiries into ourselves. But what it does mean is that we should treat with caution the ideology which tells us that scientific accounts give us the whole truth. They do not give us the whole truth even about the physical universe because they represent that world as denuded of all but its most basic properties. Even less do they give us the whole truth about the human world, because they inevitably treat its inhabitants (that is, us) as if they were not really persons.

In the latter case particularly, this means that scientific accounts are going to be radically incomplete. This is because we think of human beings as agents, as initiators of at least some of their actions. If they are really initiators of actions, then the actions in question cannot be understood as having been brought about completely by purely physical chains of causes. If human agency is to mean anything substantial, then from the point of view of physics our behaviour must be under- determined. There must be room for some force other than those admitted in physics.

To those who believe that the whole of reality can be explained and predicted in scientific terms this will be a scandalous proposition. They will say that such a notion breaches the principle of the conservation of energy. It looks as though physical events, in this case bodily movements, are being initiated or controlled by forces other than those which are dealt with in the physical sciences, those that define our understanding of energy. So where do these extra-physical inputs of energy come from?

This question is found in pretty well every contemporary discussion of the topics of consciousness and human agency, but it rests on a misconception. The misconception is, once again, that physics can explain everything, in this case all physical movements, and that all energy is that which is subject to the laws of physics. But let us suppose that there are different levels of reality. Let us suppose that the powers and mode of existence of an animal or a human being are different from those of a stone or even of the atoms which go to make up the living conscious being.

For those not already committed to some physical conservation of energy view, these would not be unreasonable suppositions. They would certainly make sense of what appears to be the case, and what is otherwise so hard to explain, namely the fact that animals and human beings do behave and experience the world in ways quite different from stones and atoms: they have conscious experience. That experience seems at times to bring about changes in the physical world, as when an animal does something because it feels pain, or I go to the shops because I have decided to do so.

Human beings are not just conscious. We are also self-movers, initiators of activity, free agents. So is there, from the physical point of view, an excess of energy which enables us to act on what we experience and what we decide to do? It might initially be brought in from outside and stored in the human being or animal, insofar as something of the sort is true of animals. But in the case of the human being acting freely, at least, what happens to the energy, once stored, cannot be explained in terms of unbroken chains of physical causality. From the point of view of physics, there will be a break, a point at which something happens where the impulse for it happening comes from outside the purview of physics.

It may be that, from the physical point of view, there is some randomness or indeterminacy at the quantum level where the choice kicks in. But that does not mean that there is not some determinate explanation at some other level. Human choice is not a matter of randomness, of a particle going one way or another with no explanation at all. Quantum theory is, of course, full of randomnesses of this sort, and within the terms of the theory no explanation for a particle's going one way rather than another can be given. But if free human action does exploit quantum level randomness, this does not mean that there is no explanation for the actions which supervene on these physically random processes: it is just that the explanation is not to be found in physics.

But it does not come from outside the world. The impulse which initiates free action, which, as it were, pushes the particle this way rather than that, comes very much from inside the world. It comes from the person who is acting, who is made up of physical bits, but whose activity is not reducible to the activity of his or her physical bits considered apart from their participation in the life of the whole person. The impulse comes specifically from his or her choice, which at the personal level is not indeterminate at all. This choice can normally be given a perfectly good explanation in terms of the reasons which have swayed the agent, issuing in the conviction that, all things considered, this rather than that is the best way to act on this occasion.

All this is something we know perfectly well from within our experience. And if it cannot, as I believe, be accounted for in terms of science, this is because the external view of science does not capture the whole of reality. Some of what happens and what exists can be understood only from within the perspective of agents, particularly their conscious experience and their choices.

It would be natural to describe the contrast in terms of a distinction between subjective and objective – natural but misleading, given that (science again!) people are almost bound to conclude that the 'subjective' features of the world are less real than the 'objective'. But they are not. Experience and choice are just as real as matter and forces, and they influence matter and forces, as well as being influenced by them.

And so we come back to the key point. Science sets out to describe the world from no particular point of view. It sets out to describe the world as if the objects in it did not have points of view, and act as they do because of forces impinging on them from outside. That indeed is its strength. It attempts to describe things as they act and react quite independently of human or any other type of experience.

In the main, science describes the world as it has gone on and will go on quite apart from what we or any other sentient beings do or think. And where beings are admitted to have conscious experience, this experience will be reduced to the physical processes which underlie it. In the scientific account, experiences play no essential role in the causal chains which determine what happens in the physical world. Consciousness is treated as merely epiphenomenal: that is, it is seen as produced by physical causes. But it does not itself produce any physical effects. Although it might seem to us as if our conscious thoughts and experiences do produce physical effects, this is an illusion. What is really producing these effects are the physical processes which underlie the experiences.

This downplaying of the mental, as has just been said, contributed to the success of science. It was when science stopped treating things in the world as if they had their own purposes and ends that it began to progress. The progress of modern science was very much due to a conscious drive on the part of scientists to see everything in the world in terms of unbroken, mechanical chains of cause and effect. Since Darwin and since the discovery of DNA even the living world has come to be seen in terms of the interaction of blind, mechanistic drives to survive and reproduce with the physical environment, with consciousness, where it exists, simply the slave of these drives.

But that does not mean that there are not also real things which the externalist, scientific perspective cannot capture. As well as physical causes and the laws underlying them, there is for human beings and other living things a view from within. And we know from experience that this subjective perspective is not without its real effects in the physical world. So, in addition to the scientific description of the world, a complete account of the world would have to include a sense of what the experiences which constitute the various subjective perspectives were like. But that is just what cannot be done except for beings which share the same types of experiences as those had by the describers. We as humans just cannot know what the quality of experience is which is had by a horse or a bat, and they could not know what ours is like.

Ruskin once wrote that there is a science of the aspects of things as well as of their nature.[17] What he meant was that in addition to things being made up of certain atoms or vibrations of matter, they also produce such and such an effect on the eye or heart. It is doubtful that there is or could be a science, properly speaking, of aspects, if only because aspects lack just that measurability and regularity on which scientific research depends. But it is true that we lead our lives largely on the level of aspects, and we can certainly give accounts of how things seem and feel to us, and how we are guided in what we do by conscious intentions and reasons.

Bringing a scientific account of the world together with an account in terms of how things seem to us remains one of the most difficult problems confronting science and philosophy. Just how do we reconcile the bleached-out accounts of science with the lived world full of secondary qualities? How can we find room for real mental causation in a world described in terms of purely physical processes?

Faced with these intractable questions, and with the difficulty of pinning down the world of lived experience, and prone as they are to generalizations and impressed with the achievements of science, many philosophers have made the hard, measurable, law-driven picture of science the touchstone of reality. But this is a mistake, and not merely because in the life which we lead scientific accounts will always be displaced by our sense that we are indeed agents and that our experience does indeed reveal genuine features of the world.

We must also remember that science itself is a point of view, with no better claim to a monopoly on truth than any other successful and well-entrenched point of view. Science does reveal much about the physical basis of the world, and the regularities which prevail at that level. As far as it goes, it is true, but it is not the whole truth. It achieves its successes – which are manifold – precisely insofar as it discounts the world of human experience, and the world as revealed in human experience.

So it is hardly surprising if science paints a picture of the world in which experience is downgraded and explained away. It could hardly do otherwise, given the framework in which it works – or rather, in which scientists work. For despite the impersonal way in which scientists typically present their results, what science is and the standpoints it adopts remain at least in part the results of human choice. Paradoxical, then, if the upshot of this choice is to deny the effectiveness of human choice. Paradoxical, perhaps, but hardly surprising given the self-denying ordinances under which scientists operate.

It would be possible to say a lot more about the institution of science, and the sociological and human factors which influence its proceedings, the choices which determine just what is studied and researched, and so on. But this is not the place for any of that, interesting and important as it is, neither is it necessary for our purposes. What is necessary for our purposes is to appreciate that science is a human activity, and one which deliberately abstracts from much that is real. So science should not be treated as if it is the sole arbiter of what there really is – and that is all we need to establish at this point.

7 Aesthetics

The impact of science is to shatter the world of appearance. Secondary qualities are demoted or dismissed altogether as illusory. Conscious experience is downplayed, treated as a literally useless epiphenomenon. In the ultimate resort, it is to be eliminated from science altogether.

But, as we have already suggested, none of this is sustainable. It is not just that the aspects of life with which science is dispensing are useful in various ways. More, we care about how things seem to us. We care about the colours and sounds with which we are surrounded, and how things – and people – look and feel. Smells are important, and so is taste. We do not have to be gourmets or addicted to exotic perfumes to recognize this. The experiences life affords us are not simply ways of gaining information about the environment: they are important to us in and for themselves. They are essential ingredients in the quality of any life.

So, a monotonous street, unrelieved by gardens or buildings of elegance is profoundly depressing to live in, even though it may have perfectly adequate space, cleanliness and light. And so is an untidy or undecorated room. A house is not just a shelter, but something everyone attempts to prettify, according to their taste. Judging by what we know of early mankind, this has been so since prehistoric times. Ornament is not crime, or, if it is, we are all criminals, including the architects who imposed this inhuman doctrine on buildings they themselves did not occupy.

We surround ourselves with pictures and music, not to give information about faraway places or people's states of mind, but because we like how they look and sound. Style plays a greater or a lesser part in all our lives, even in the lives of those of us who claim to be unaffected by fashion (which is usually a style statement in itself).

It is often said that taste is not to be argued about, and that matters of taste simply reflect personal preference or some transient social consensus. But that is surely false. The arguments we all engage in about the virtues of competing tastes are among the fiercest and most bitterly contested. We know, deep down, that these things do matter. They are important in themselves. They are also closely connected to other important values.

Aesthetic considerations – those to do with beauty, style and taste – play a huge part in all our lives. One is tempted to say that once basic needs have been satisfied, aesthetic considerations play an increasingly predominant role in the lives of human beings. But this underestimates the need for the aesthetic. Even in the poorest of circumstances people have a yearning for order and beauty. This yearning will reveal itself in the ways they organize their shelter, prepare their meals, dress themselves and respond to natural sights and sounds. Aesthetics pervades human life, even at the most basic level and even in fulfilling the most basic physical needs.

In view of this, it is surprising that the reflection on aesthetic value plays only a small and rather unregarded role in contemporary philosophy. This may be because most philosophers, like most of their contemporaries, underestimate the extent and importance of the aesthetic in all our lives. It may also be because of a widespread feeling that judgements about beauty and style are pretty arbitrary, just expressions of personal or social preference, grounded in nothing objective. And it may also be because the notion of beauty – traditionally the central point of any inquiry into aesthetic value – is itself unfashionable.

It is certainly unfashionable if one takes as one's guide fashionable contemporary art, as a visit to Tate Modern in London or to the Museum of Modern Art in New York will confirm. If we look at the works exhibited there and the explanations offered for them, contemporary high art is about all sorts of things. It is about politics, ideas, shock, feminism, gender, identity, space, time, ways of seeing, memory, the transgression of boundaries and much else besides, including the very notion of high art. But one thing it is not about, or about only incidentally, is beauty.

Analogous points could be made about contemporary architecture, music, dance and writing, and about large swathes of popular culture. To ages other than our own, this would have seemed a strange, if not remarkable state of affairs. Art and music, architecture, poetry, theatre and classical ballet might be about a lot of things, but one thing they have all been concerned with traditionally is beauty. Maybe this was never true of all art all the time, but it certainly used to be true of most art, most of the time.

In our culture as a whole we are shy of beauty, and this is no less true of the writings of contemporary philosophers. On the whole they are unwilling or even embarrassed to discuss beauty or to make judgements about the role aesthetic values ought to play in our lives.

There is a one good, though not conclusive, reason for the philosophical neglect of the notion of beauty. It is that to describe a work of art or a piece of nature as beautiful is often rather unhelpful. It does not point to any precise aspect of what is being praised. It can amount to little more than a form of empty emoting, a generalized and undirected gush of approval.

On the other hand, in a more restricted sense, to call something beautiful is to say that it has a kind of superior prettiness, which would rule out the tragic and the sublime and many other tougher but nevertheless desirable characteristics. Clearly a notion of this sort could not be the central concept of aesthetics. It would not be worth any great amount of argument or discussion. It would certainly not have elicited from Rilke the thought that

> **beauty's nothing
> but beginning of Terror we're still just able to bear,
> and why we adore it so is because it serenely
> disdains to destroy us.**
>
> (First Duino Elegy, lines 4–7)[18]

Reassured by Rilke, let us spend a little time considering beauty as the central positive notion of aesthetics, that which we apply to those works and scenes which move us forcefully and positively, and which for that very reason we find worth preserving or having or re-visiting. In examining this notion we might then be enabled some conclusions about the nature and status of our aesthetic sense, and also about what it tells us about ourselves and about the world.

Perhaps the most obvious thing to say about things which are beautiful is that beautiful things attract. They inspire love, as has been said, and they do this because they have qualities such as nobility, grace, balance, harmony, dignity, humanity, pathos, wit, elegance, grandeur and sympathy, rather than their opposites. Or if they have negative qualities such as dreariness, ungainliness, clumsiness, barbarity, discordance, terror, aggression, viciousness, cruelty, sentimentality, irony and ugliness, these are outweighed by positive qualities so as to produce an ultimately harmonious whole. We are all familiar with the 'terrible beauty' of tragedy, of *Hamlet*, say, or of *The Oresteia*. We can distinguish the impact of these works from plays and films in which degradation and horror are revelled in, with no relieving aspirations or elevating framework, with no attempt to reconcile us to the necessity of what we have just witnessed.

This does not, of course, mean that every work of art has to aim at beauty. Some may be intentionally horrific or horrible, in order to respond to horrific or horrible themes or circumstances. They can be very effective as works of art. Equally, though in our unreligious age more problematic, there can be works of art which treat horrific events as tragic, as part of some cosmic order, rather than as merely horrible. We will return to both these possibilities, but before doing so we need to consider three purely formal characteristics of a judgement to the effect that something is beautiful. And in doing this we will be following the analysis offered by Kant in his *Critique of Judgement*.

According to Kant a favourable aesthetic judgement – of

which holding that a part of nature or a work of art is beautiful is the central example – will be disinterested, universal and non-cognitive. We will consider what each of these claims amounts to.

Disinterestedness means that in admiring something for its beauty, we are admiring it for what it is in itself, and not for some other purpose the object might serve. We can thus distinguish between two possible responses to a work of art on the part of its owner, say. He might value his painting because of what it is worth, or he might simply admire what seems to him to be its outstanding beauty. He might, of course, combine both attitudes, but what the disinterested-ness of the aesthetic judgement means is that in calling a work beautiful one is abstracting from further purposes it might serve, such as enriching its owner. One is admiring it simply for its appearance.

But this does not mean that in seeing something as beautiful, all we are to take into consideration are its purely formal features, its abstract geometry, so to speak. There can be a type of beauty in purely abstract patterns and sounds, but beauty is by no means restricted to such things, nor does the disinterestedness of beauty imply that it is.

In admiring something simply for its appearance, we are not debarred from thinking about what it is and about how things of that type are supposed to look. Once we start thinking of something as a beautiful x, where x is some definite type of thing, we will actually have to take such matters into account. So, if a racehorse is commended for its beauty, it will look like a racehorse rather than like a dog. It will be beautiful in the manner of racehorses. Features which might be admirable in a King Charles spaniel would detract from the beauty of a horse, were they to be found in one, however many races it won.

Disinterestedness characterizes my appreciation of the beauty of Desert Orchid, say, because I am focusing simply on how he appears, and how his appearance is an admirable combination of strength, elegance, speed, grace, nobility, and so on. I am not for the moment bothered about how much he is worth, how much I might have won or lost on him, who his owner and trainer are, or any other similarly important but aesthetically extraneous matters.

Recognizing that beauty is not purely abstract is important because it means that in making judgements of beauty we often have to take into account more than the pure form of the object. We may have to consider its function in relation to its form (as in the racehorse example), or we may have to consider the broader moral and human implications of what is being depicted. Thus, viewed simply as patterns and colours and paint, it might be possible to find a Francis Bacon canvas admirable, beautiful even, yet profoundly ugly once it is realized just what is being depicted.

So the disinterestedness of beauty does not imply a purely formal attitude to the beautiful. But it does mean that in being attracted to something for its beauty, we are admiring it for what it is in itself. We are putting to one side its cost or its value as propaganda or its therapeutic potential or its effectiveness in stimulating its audience to sexual licence or drug-taking.

The beautiful is also universal. In judging something to be beautiful we are implying that anyone who studies the object with sufficient care, patience and attention will agree. Faced with the prevalence of relativism in all matters, but particularly on aesthetic matters, this might seem an extraordinary claim. Do not some people just like *Neighbours* and others Shakespeare; some Keats and others Bob Dylan and others again Oasis; some Poussin and others Damien Hirst; and isn't that all there is to it? Isn't the claim that there is more just out-dated snobbery, a conspiracy of a narrow privileged élite to exclude the majority, something which has no place in a modern, democratic and multicultural world?

The first point to make is that the universality of the aesthetic judgement does not imply that anyone or everyone will actually agree with any particular judgement which is made. What it does mean, though, is that such judgements are more than merely expressions of preference. In saying that one painting is beautiful and another ugly, one is saying something about the paintings, something about their respective merits and faults. And that is something which can be explained, argued about and discussed. It is also something on which people can be right or wrong.

Agreement may not always be reached. Aesthetic discussion is not science and does not have measurable quantities, but at least we are in the realm of thoughtful, reasoned conversation. It is not like me liking dark chocolate and you hating it, about which there really is nothing more to be said, except perhaps about the physiology of our taste buds. Aesthetic judgement is more like our reaction to those contemporaries of Beethoven who were unable to appreciate the merits of his late quartets. Leaving philosophical prejudice aside, do we not in practice think that they were missing something that is actually there, in the works? Equally, and in some ways more striking, from the distance of a century or more it is easy for us to perceive that those Victorians who regarded G. F. Watts as the new Leonardo, Makart as the Michelangelo of his time and Meyerbeer as a supreme composer were seeing qualities in the work that are simply not there.

The point about temporal distance is crucial. Fashion is very difficult to eliminate when considering work of one's own time. Everyone is more or less prisoner of the prejudices of their own age. (Doubtless we have our own Watts, Makarts and Meyerbeers, even if to some of us the Hirsts, Freuds and Lloyd Webbers seem infinitely more sophisticated.)

Distance lends not enchantment, but perspective. And in considering works from another age or time, one is benefiting from a multiplicity of viewpoints. One is moving to a more inclusive, more universal frame of reference. The point has been well and memorably put by Hume:

> The same Homer, who pleased at Athens and Rome two thousand years ago, is still admired at Paris and London. All the changes of climate, government, religion and language have not been able to obscure his glory. Authority or prejudice may be able to give a temporary vogue to a bad poet or orator; but his reputation will never be durable or general. When his compositions are examined by posterity or foreigners, the enchantment is dissipated and his faults appear in their true colours. On the contrary, the longer his works endure, and the more wide they are spread, the more sincere is the admiration which they meet with.[20]

Hume is right. Despite all the scepticism there is on the objectivity of beauty, there is convergence of judgement over time. We can and do appreciate Homer and Aeschylus, Phidias and Praxiteles, Virgil and Dante, despite vast differences of time, place, society and viewpoint. Most of us are not immune to the attractions of Islamic architecture, Chinese calligraphy, Dravidian temple art and Aztec sculpture, strange as such things may be to us, and even though few of us will ever do more than scratch their surface.

In practice, then, most of us do believe in the universality of the aesthetic, as the mantra of 'celebrating the richness and diversity of our multicultural society' in its confused way suggests. Even if overlaid with relativism and denigration of 'dead white males', the multicultural message is a hopeful one, for it testifies to the possibility of communication and understanding across countries, languages and times. In metaphorically travelling through space and time, those who get beyond the superficial stage of cultural tourism will begin to acquire the knowledge to make comparative judgements of the aesthetic value of what is perceived, whether what is perceived is 'theirs' and of 'ours'. Or rather there will be no more 'theirs' and 'ours', but a sense of an underlying universality of humanity and of humanity's works.

After disinterestedness and universality we come to the non-cognitiveness of the aesthetic. Contained in this rather unfortunate phrase is the surely acceptable insight that knowledge of the aesthetic qualities of a thing, positive or negative, requires personal acquaintance with that thing. That is to say, there is no rule which could determine whether something is beautiful in advance of knowing the work, that is in advance of seeing, hearing or reading it. Only someone who is personally acquainted with a work of art will be in a position to expatiate on its qualities. Merely reading about it or being told about it or seeing a reproduction will not be enough.

For example, one might judge, as Ruskin did, that in a Veronese painting what would in other hands be a mass of 'trivial and even ludicrous detail' in no way detracts from the nobleness of the whole.[21] Ruskin was writing about Veronese's 'Presentation of the Queen of Sheba' (now in Turin), but the same point could be made of 'The Family of Darius Before Alexander' (in London) or 'The Marriage Feast at Cana' (in the Louvre), and of many other of Veronese's great set pieces.

It is not just that in order to consider the truth or otherwise of Ruskin's judgement, one would have actually to see the painting or paintings in question, though it is partly that. There is also the question of the amount of detail which might be trivial and ludicrous even in the hands of Veronese. Just how much would that be? Another couple of animals, perhaps, lurking at the bottom of the canvas, which unlike the ones there, might begin to deflect attention from the solemn and moving events going on in the main body of the painting? What is it about the composition, structure, colour and narrative grasp exemplified in a Veronese set-piece which preserves balance in the midst of all the detail there is? Why, in other hands, would that amount of detail have rendered the subject-matter wholly un-unified, in the unpainterly sense a mere narrative, hardly more than photographic reportage? (Think, for example, of Frith's 'Derby Day'.)

The point is that there is no general answer to these questions. There is no rule which the critic can lay down in advance to adjudicate. The only recourse is to appeal to the precise nature of the composition of the paintings, and how they culminate in the particular experience afforded by 'The Family of Darius' as opposed to that afforded by 'Derby Day'.

The way aesthetic judgements are rooted in experience and the absence of general rules determining their outcomes is part of what is meant by non-cognitiveness in this context. But Kant meant something else as well. He meant that aesthetic judgements are ineliminably subjective. They can be nothing other than subjective, as he said. They are not true or false. They do not refer to real properties of the world; but, rather like the scientific treatment of secondary qualities, they are actually about feelings and experiences produced in us when we perceive things.

The subjectivity of the aesthetic can be reconciled with its universality because Kant believed that we share a common human nature. He supposed that as a result we human beings would tend to converge in our aesthetic judgements. But the doctrine is none the more palatable for that. Take a typical aesthetic judgement. Someone says that a Beethoven scherzo is rumbustuous and good-humoured, as opposed to sardonic and sepulchral (which might be true of a Mahler scherzo). It falsifies both logic and experience to think that he is talking about feelings in his breast rather than about properties objectively present in the movement and which are crucial in determining the overall effect of the work as a whole – its beauty, if you like. And it is highly significant that judgements of this sort can be supported – or undermined – by appeal to the detail of the score.

Those who follow Kant in denying the objectivity of aesthetic judgements are probably influenced by a reductive account of rationality. They think that only scientific judgements can be true or false because only properties which are measurable and observations which can be made by any observer (even a mechanical one) are to count. Everything else is consigned to the dustbin of the subjective. It is this thought which has influenced so many philosophers to think of the non-measurable properties of morality and the aesthetic as belonging to the realm of 'mere' feeling. But, as has just been observed, when we come to look at actual moral and aesthetic judgements we do take ourselves to be speaking of real properties; beauty, ugliness and more specific aesthetic properties are in the world and in things, even if, like secondary qualities, they can be perceived only by human beings and creatures with similar make-ups.

The analysis of the aesthetic judgement as disinterested, universal and non-cognitive has been rather abstract and formal. But having followed its detail will help us to see why, in art at least, beauty has been marginalized in recent decades. It is because artists and patrons have ceased to be interested in art which is disinterested and universal. They have also favoured art whose point is not to be perceived, but thought about or serving some function other than the aesthetic.

Speaking of a new type of museum – and by extension of the new type of art which might fill it – the philosopher and art critic Arthur Danto has written:

> Their conception of art is very much one of interestedness, and is not at all universal. The art, like the museum, speaks in a special way to the group whose art and museum it is. To experience the art is from the start to have an interest . . . (an) interest that has as its object the furtherance of the group to which one belongs. The art is there for the sake of that interest. It follows that, from this perspective, the primary concern of art (not the art, notice) is not that it be beautiful – or in any case – its being so is secondary. It follows further that artistic experience is not aesthetic either. It is instead political and instrumental . . . Needless to say, the art made present to the visitors related to it through interest need not be great art by universal criteria at all.[22]

Danto is referring to museums and art devoted to various identities – ethnic, gender, political and the like. But there is also plenty of such work in museums devoted to art in general. Critics have noticed, as Danto himself has observed, that such work is not always of the highest quality. But to say that is to miss its point. Its point is precisely not to attain the disinterestedness of beauty, nor its universality. Its whole and only point is the furtherance of one's group or cause, and that is how it should be judged.

So it is not surprising if work which attempts to avoid two of the conditions for beauty (universality and disin-terestedness) often fails to be beautiful. Nor is it surprising that artists aiming at some cause or other often use means which would normally be regarded as militating against the beautiful, and deliberately flout canons of symmetry, taste, elegance, balance and harmony. They actually want their work to be ugly, distorted and offensive, in order for it to fulfil the broadly political purpose they have for it.

Let us leave aside the irony that the state itself is the main sponsor of artistic work aimed at undermining the current social order. There is also the fact that many of those involved in producing and promoting this work would be quick to assert that in art political servitude means bad art. They would probably be thinking of the art of the 1930s, produced in accordance with the wishes of the dictatorships of Russia, Germany and Italy. But what we see now is that aesthetics can also be subverted by politics of a non-dictatorial, liberational kind, as it can by art produced for other interested purposes, such as the pop music aimed at stimulating people to indulge in sexual activity and drug abuse.

In all these cases we have art whose interest is not to be contemplated disinterestedly, and not to appeal over time to people of all places and backgrounds, so it is hardly surprising if it is mostly not beautiful. What is surprising is that so much art of our time does not even try to be beautiful. It no longer shares the ambition of much of the art of the past.

But, it might be said, much of the art of the past was religious. Does religious art aim to be universal and disinterested in the appropriate sense? And if not, is this not a problem for our analysis of beauty, as most people, whether believers or not, undeniably find beauty in the great Gothic cathedrals of England and France, and in Bach's Passions and church cantatas, to take only the most obvious examples of religious art of high achievement.

That in itself suggests that universality may not be a problem here. At least some religious art – the beautiful stuff

– does cut across time and place. But what about disinterest-edness? Are these things disinterested in the relevant sense?

It must be admitted that some religious art is very preacherly and obviously didactic and devotional, just like feminist or socialist agit-prop. But equally it would probably not be generally regarded as beautiful either. Religious art, though, does not have to be indoctrinatory or obviously animated by missionary zeal. It can be, and often is, contem-plative, in the sense of being simply for the glory of God, as would be said. And here, there could be both truth and the disinterestedness characteristic of the truly beautiful, with things there for their own sake and for the sake of their beauty.

Religious commission and subject matter do not, then, of themselves impede an artist in pursuing the virtues of his or her art. The very dynamic of the religious impulse can lead artists to cut themselves off from considerations of purely human motivation. Indeed a certain interpretation of religious insight – one which accepts the world and humanity in all its light and shadow, without anxiety or lust or spite or remorse – could actually contribute positively in an artist's work to the disinterestedness and universality central to aesthetic beauty.

We have dwelt at some length on the way in which much contemporary art repudiates any drive towards Kantian dis-interestedness and universality. But there is another way in which beauty can be avoided by the artist flouting the third Kantian requirement, non-cognitiveness. That is to say, art can be produced whose point is not the experience it produces in the perceiver, but rather its adherence to some doctrine whose point is that there should be something about the work other than what can be directly perceived.

There are, in the art of the last hundred years or so, at least two tendencies which militate against the requirement that what counts first and foremost in a work is the experience it produces on the perceiver. There is first the doctrine that what is crucial is some underlying – and hence imperceptible – structure rather than the perceivable surface of the work. Perhaps the most famous version of this doctrine was serialism in music, but a similar tendency is present in the architectural doctrine of functionality. Both these not unconnected doctrines represent a deliberate downgrading of the immediately perceivable in favour of something graspable only in abstract by the intellect.

And therein lies their difficulty. What comes to dominate in composing a piece of music or in designing a building is not what can be perceived, but – it would be said – something far more important. There is in these doctrines an inbuilt snobbishness against the merely perceptible and also against the widely appreciated, a snobbishness neatly encapsulated by the dictum of the architect Adolf Loos that ornament is crime.

There are a few works of musical serialism of great beauty and of wide appeal, Berg's Violin Concerto being among the most notable. This, as anyone who has heard it will know, is a work of haunting and elegiac beauty. But this is because of how it sounds, and not because of its adherence to the strictures of serialism. In fact, it does not sound like a piece of serialism, which prompts the conclusion that its conformity to the principles of serialism is irrelevant to the way we hear it. The piece is a triumph of Berg's musicality over theoretical constraint.

Where in music the rigours of the twelve-note scale took

precedence over appearance, in architecture it was function-ality. Function was supposed to take precedence over appearance, particularly over functionally unnecessary ornament. Proponents of this doctrine tended to ignore the point that ornament, while not always holding buildings up, often served the humanly essential function of giving buildings a comfortable feel or could even make them look beautiful. That they ignored aesthetic function in this way shows the narrowness of their view of function, which did not even go as far as recommending that a building ought to look like what it was intended to be (a church, a school, a house, or whatever).

It was rather that you were supposed to dispense with any preconceptions about what buildings of particular types were supposed to look like. Instead, appearance was to be determined by analysis of the functions the building was supposed to serve, which were in themselves to be discovered by a quasi-scientific account of human need and by how best the technology of the time could produce what was needed. (For example, human beings needed x amount of light, y amount of space and z amount of heating in their living accommodation, and modern building techniques and reinforced concrete could supply these needs most efficiently in apartment blocks of such and such dimensions.) In all this analysis and 'research into function' aesthetic properties were to play at most a subordinate role.

Were supposed to. In fact there was an aesthetic underlying architectural functionalism. It was the aesthetic in which anything pertaining to the beautiful or to the traditional tastes of old-fashioned human beings was mere clutter, to be ruthlessly eliminated by the new architectural rationalism, a rationalism not unlike Schoenberg's serialism in music in both motivation and effects. (This aesthetic rationalism also has its analogue in the equally dehumanizing moral philosophies of the twentieth century, which, as we have already seen, also attempted to reconstruct systems of practice afresh on a very narrow theoretical basis.)

In the architectural realm the upshot has been homes and public buildings built on reductively functionalist principles, and as such widely disliked by those whose aesthetic needs have been disregarded in so cavalier a fashion. The conclusion must surely be that in aiming at theory and function, rather than having a care for the all-important appearance of things, art will make the achievement of beauty that much more unlikely.

But so will it if the aim is taken to be to convey an idea or – as arts bureaucrats like to put it – to challenge the preconceptions of the audience. This 'theory art' reaches its *reductio ad absurdum* in the joke slogans of the American artist Jenny Holzer which, once seen, do not need to be seen again (or more accurately which, once heard, do not need to be seen at all). But quasi-philosophic challenge is routinely trotted out as the aim and justification of a host of contemporary works of art, from the medicine cabinets and pickled animals of Damien Hirst, to Rachel Whiteread's casts of the underside of chairs, to the homosexual scatology of Gilbert and George, to the Jeff Koons' vacuum cleaners and pornographic photographs, through to Tracy Emin's bed and life, the artist's life now itself a work of art, no matter how squalid, immature and disedifying.

In these cases, too, there is really no need to see the

objects in question, or, even if there is an initial visual impact, it rapidly diminishes in impact and interest, much as the typical arresting advertisement and for much the same reason. People come into a gallery full of modern installation art and, once they have got the idea, are at a loss to know what to look at. Quite the reverse happens when they examine a Monet or a Renoir, for example, where fascination with and interest in the surface and what is seen in it appears virtually endless. Part of the attraction of great art undoubtedly lies in its seeming inexhaustibility, the way one individual can return to the same work over and over again without exhausting its interest and the way a single work can remain a focus of fascination for different people and different times.

There are, then, aspects of fashion in contemporary art which militate against the achievement of beauty. These are a repudiation of disinterestedness in favour of work which serves some political or therapeutic purpose, an emphasis on art as the embodiment of particular identities, and a focus on non-perceptual properties, such as an imperceptible underlying structure or the satisfaction of functional demands in a utilitarian sense. These are all ways in which works of art and architecture can and frequently do flout the requirements for the beautiful correctly identified by Kant.

But these are purely formal requirements. They tell us nothing about the content of the work. A work could be dis-interested, aiming at universality and what could actually be perceived, and still fail to be beautiful. It could, of course, fail because of incompetence on the part of its creator. But, more interestingly, it could fail because its creator might have wanted it to be ugly or discordant or raucous or unsettling. And he may have wanted it to be these things because of some view he has about our time or situation. After Auschwitz, it might be asked, should we even be aiming at beauty?

Presumably the point of this question is not that Auschwitz was in the twentieth century uniquely horrible and wicked, which it was not, but that it was a horror and an evil carried out by a nation which prided itself on its culture and its cultivation of beauty, and in the case of music at least rightly so. To this, one obvious reply, and one which would doubtless have commended itself to Goethe and Schiller, would be that, if true, it makes the Holocaust that much worse.

A more considered answer would have to consider German history and character in the round. Love of music and a devotion to the classical past was, after all, only one element in a complex story, and Hitler aside, not a highly significant element in the mentality of most of the perpetrators of the Holocaust. Apart from more obviously political elements, the story also included a deliberate and philosophically inspired attempt on the part of many of its leading spirits to transvalue all values and also to repudiate any sense of the unity of mankind and of the universality of moral and aesthetic judgements. In any case, the fact that beauty can co-exist with evil does not show that beauty is not a goal worth pursuing, or indeed that if properly pursued it does not have a close connection with the good.

For is it not the case that seeing things as beautiful, or certainly seeing the world as a whole as beautiful, suggests that ultimately all is, or could be, well with the world? Of course, one could be seduced by a momentary pleasure in some sight or sound without this having any more profound overtones; but the question is, what is suggested if one takes the seeking and cultivating of beauty to be a prominent motive in one's life?

According to Kant, in judging something to be beautiful, we find a harmony between our judgement and it. But how, deep down, can there be any such harmony if there is no harmony between the world and us, between us and the rest of our kind, and between our deepest yearning and our inevitable fate? How, after Darwin has revealed the natural world to be a place of waste, pointless suffering and relentless struggle, can we continue to see it as filled with beauty?

So, in short, even if there are temporary experiences of beauty, these are inevitably tinged with an almost sickly nostalgia and world-weariness, as in the final trio of *Der Rosenkavalier*. They are at best a bit of self-indulgence, a childish avoidance of what we really know to be true. But they are not serious. In other words, we won't, in our conscious and adult lives, have beauty because beauty belongs to our and mankind's infancy.

We will confront questions of the truth or otherwise of a religious attitude to the world in the next chapter, but in a post-religious age such as ours, such an attitude can come to seem all but forced on us. That so many artists and musicians seem to take it may help to explain why, when we seek beauty in art, we do not turn to works of our own time, and also why the artists of our time seem unconcerned in their work with the Kantian conditions for beauty.

But there is another possible view, and it is the view associated with Plato. It is the view that the experience of beauty itself is part of a background which elevates us, and which justifies the world.

What Plato suggests in the dialogue *Symposium* is this. The lover of beauty has his first experience of beauty in being captivated by the beauty of individual bodies. To the extent that this is an interested attraction – closely linked to desire for physical possession – it is, in Kantian terms, a pre-aesthetic experience rather than aesthetic in the full sense. It may, nevertheless, be a more realistic account of the genesis of the aesthetic sense than Kant's rather austere account, or it may simply be an irrelevance; maybe pre-adolescent children are already blessed with a keen aesthetic sense in their perception of the natural world.

Be that as it may, what is suggestive in Plato's account are the next two stages. After having had his soul plucked from his mouth by the very existence of his loved one, the aesthete begins to scan 'beauty's wide horizon'. He detaches himself from 'the slavish and illiberal devotion to the individual loveliness of a single boy' (it is a boy in Plato), and turns his eye disinterestedly to 'the open sea of beauty'. There is then a third stage in the ascent to the transcendent in which love for the beautiful transforms itself into love for something which is not physical at all.

Now, as far as aesthetics is concerned, this non-physical attraction must be a step too far. At the very least, it contravenes the requirement of non-cognitiveness, as the non-physical beauty of which Plato speaks is not experienceable. But what is illuminating in his story is the way our sense for beauty is represented as moving from intense sensual attraction, which may hardly be aesthetic at all, to a sense which diffuses itself over everything, seeking and producing beauty everywhere, and which is understood to reveal to us something about the ultimate structure of reality.

But, to come back to our earlier question, does the sense of harmony implicit in the experience of beauty point to anything fundamentally right about the world? To see things in the world and to attempt to confront our fate as beautiful is to perceive the world as not ultimately alien, and ourselves as not necessarily alienated.

So, on the Platonic account, the aesthetic sense points to and presupposes the type of ultimate harmony and meaning in the universe which are symbolized in more direct ways by religions. This is not to say that the religious sense is justified, or that our consolation in the aesthetic is not, at root, an illusion. It is not to say that aesthetic experience is not just wish fulfilment powered by the type of release which certain shapes and colours and sounds produce in the chemistry of the brain, which is how a materialistic account would analyse it.

So we come back to our age and its lack of care for the beautiful. We evidently lack the type of shared symbolic order which in previous ages has sustained artistic styles and forged aesthetic communities. Publicly we lack the type of vision, religious or otherwise, which might fill out the aesthetic sense into something intimating transcendence and meaning.

Ruskin drew a distinction between what he called aesthesis and theoria, a distinction which throws some light on our questions and on our current artistic predicament. Aesthesis is 'the mere animal consciousness of the pleasantness' which one has on perceiving something beautiful, whereas theoria is the sense that beauty has a spiritual core, that it bears witness to the glory of God. As early as 1846, and long before 'art for art's sake' became an established position, Ruskin predicted that if the arts stayed at the level of aesthesis, they would degenerate 'into mere amusement, ministers to morbid sensibilities, ticklers and fanners of the soul's sleep'.[23]

But this may not be the end of the story. The great works of art of the past, many conceived and executed quite explicitly within a transcendent framework, have a charge and a vivacity quite missing from most of the art of our day. Even as the public culture denies any such thing, many of us today have private experiences of theoria.

So perhaps the experience of the beautiful does provide a way through one of our dilemmas. It may suggest an attitude to life which is neither that of science, with its downgrading of appearance, nor that of morality with its emphasis on stern and probably unfulfillable duty and on the apparently pointless and endless suffering to which humanity is subject. For in the experience of beauty we get a sense that, despite the problems of alienation thrown up in different ways by science and morality, we are nevertheless at home in the world.

By 'at home', I mean that the world is not just the blind, random, humanly indifferent entity described by modern science. It is in some sense responsive to our concerns. Consciousness (our consciousness) does take us to the essence of the world, and meaning and intelligibility are not simply imposed by us on a world which is ultimately meaningless and indifferent.

From a perspective of this sort, even if we do not believe in an afterlife, there can, as there was for the ancient Greeks, be a form of tragedy which sees the fate of human beings as part of a cycle of cosmic justice, in which our finite lives have their place. As Ruskin put it, the blood of heroes, though poured out onto the ground, rises into hyacinthine flowers, and the gods whom they had never ceased to love, come down to love them.

Aesthetic experience can, then, suggest a type of feeling and a depth of meaning beyond the everyday. Still, there may be nothing which really answers that feeling or corresponds to that meaning. There may be no God or gods, no cosmic justice, no true tragedy, only meaningless death as part of a life driven by meaningless biological urges and imperatives – in which case aesthetic experience has no more significance than a warm bath of Prozac or some other way of affecting the chemistry of the brain. In which case, too, art might just as well be a wallowing in degradation, a quickly forgotten 'sensation' or a piece of quirky sub-philosophical conceptualism, whereby the artist (yet again) calls into 'question' art itself or some aspect of our contemporary normality.

On the other hand, the experiences one has in seeing *King Lear* or in listening to Beethoven's Op. 132 do not feel in the least like having a bath or the effects of taking a pill. In Lear the experience is that, despite the appearance to the world of Goneril and Regan, Lear and Cordelia do not die like dogs, but with meaning and a certain pathos and even dignity. In the case of Beethoven, we have the *Heiliger Dankgesang*, praise for the spirit who harmonizes and elevates the universe. In both cases we feel ourselves close to Rilke's beginning of terror, serenely disdaining to destroy us, close though it may come to it. In both cases we are a million miles from the tawdriness, ephemerality and lack of nobility of most contemporary art and literature.

For those whose horizons are bounded by materialism or physicalism, none of the drift of the last few paragraphs will begin to be credible: it may not even make sense. But if it does not, both art and beauty are likely to be transformed. More precisely, art as a quest for universal and disinterested experiences of beauty will become problematic if the world can sustain no sense of the beautiful beyond aesthesis. Aesthesis itself will look increasingly like a temporary and indulgent retreat from the reality of our condition. And so in our art we get the shark in formaldehyde, the soiled bed, the close-up of the artist's orifices, the theatre of cruelty and perversion and novels wallowing in self-pity and the author's streams of consciousness untroubled by any reality principle. Not art, maybe, in the sense of the past; but neither an unavailing attempt to escape from the meaninglessness of existence.

But even so, for some art, particularly the art of the past will continue to point to a sense that there is in the universe a power which works towards the good and gives the universe and our existence a meaning beyond that provided by science. It suggests further that in our conscious experience we can link ourselves to that power, and that we do so not by denying our embodiment, but precisely by using it. All this, of course, raises the ultimate question: is there any such power? This is the subject of the next chapter.

8 **Religion**

Traditionally wisdom had religious connotations, and in the popular mind it still does. What seekers after wisdom are often looking for is some indication that there is more to our existence than the birth, copulation and death of biological necessity. It is the function of 'wisdom' to supply this indication, typically by means of some revelation or sacred teaching.

But they will look in vain if they expect anything of this sort from contemporary philosophy. In part this is to do with the materialism and scientism of much contemporary philosophy. But it is also a result of philosophy's self-denying ordinance, obeyed even by philosophers expressing a religious view of life: that philosophy, *qua* philosophy, is to stick to what can be ascertained by human reason, unaided by any kind of revelation or religious teaching.

This in itself is not enough to support any kind of materialism. After all, from Socrates and Plato onwards, right up to at least the turn of the nineteenth century, for the most part philosophy had been by no means hostile to religious impulses: rather the contrary in fact. Just as fast as some eighteenth- and nineteenth-century philosophers undermined traditional religious conceptions, other philosophers (and sometimes even the same ones) tried desperately to articulate ways of keeping the religious impulse alive without reliance on traditional faith and dogma.

But philosophy as 'spilt religion', as it was disparagingly called, itself flowed away in the twentieth century, as the subject took on a harder edge. What was regarded as woolly speculation gave way to hard-nosed preoccupations with science and political structures. Nor could it be said that the pious were especially comforted by philosophical attempts to construct versions of religion which dispensed with reference to most of the essential beliefs of Christianity.

In this they could be seen as echoing Pascal's complaint against any philosophical meddling in religious life and faith. Pascal contrasted the God of the philosophers with the God of Abraham, Isaac and Jacob. The one was a living power to whom man could relate, who saved those who had belief and who demanded wholehearted worship and commitment. The other, the philosophical God, was a timeless abstraction – remote, unchanging and perfect. This God was a mere concept rather than the jealous, personal God of the Old Testament, whose Son became man and redeemed us in the New.

Pascal's complaint was levelled against the so-called natural theology of the medieval scholastic philosophers, such as St Thomas Aquinas, and their Jesuit successors in his own time. What was here attempted was the proof of God's existence and speculation about his nature from pure reason. The trouble with it from Pascal's point of view was that the being whose existence and nature was demonstrated was that of Aristotelian metaphysics rather than that of a living faith.

Nevertheless the traditional proofs of God's existence cannot be simply dismissed, either by believers who find their upshot too impersonal, or by materialist philosophers who find their reasoning unpersuasive. The truth is that, even if they do not actually prove anything, they do point to aspects of existence which, whatever one finally concludes, are bound to remain mysterious. What I want to suggest is that, even so, in a contest between materialistic atheism and some kind of religious-cum-theistic view, the materialistic conclusion leaves even more mysteries than a view which sees reason and consciousness as part of the essence of the universe.

We will start by looking at the two most familiar proofs of the existence of God. These are the first-cause argument and the argument from design. Both have taken a heavy battering from philosophers, particularly over the past two to three hundred years; but even now many people find one or both of them intuitively plausible.

The first-cause argument focuses on the underlying reason for the existence of anything. It is often expressed in temporal terms, in terms of the origins of the universe, but, as we will see, this is not crucial to it.

Why does anything exist? This is a highly ambiguous question. Why does any particular thing exist? Or, why does anything at all exist?

To take the first question first. Why does any particular thing exist? Why does this cup exist? Why do I exist? Why does the tree outside my window exist?

We can, of course, answer, more or less adequately, each of these questions. The cup exists because it was produced in such and such a factory. I exist because of my parents. The tree exists because a seed fell or was planted where it is, the seed was watered and sustained, the tree was enabled to grow to maturity, etc.

But, it will be said, each of these answers, even if adequate as far as it goes, only takes us to other similar questions about the causes of the causes. Why does the factory exist? Why did my parents exist? How did the seed come into being, and how is it that the conditions for its growing and maturing came to have that sort of outcome?

Once again, at least in principle, answers can be given. But it will be obvious that, as the story develops, we are led to postulate earlier and earlier causes, and also to develop accounts of more and more general and basic properties of matter itself. Ultimately, if the story could be taken back that far, we will come to the Big Bang, the point at which the first bit of matter suddenly came into being and, with it, we are told, to the laws which govern the behaviour and development of everything that there is. And so, once again in principle, and leaving aside complications arising from the physically unpredictable operation of human freedom, it looks as if it might be possible to tell some story about how the present state of the universe, including me, the tree and my cup, all came about as a result of things which happened at the Big Bang itself.

But even if this were so, a deep problem would remain. What caused the Big Bang? And how, if matter were created at the Big Bang, could something (matter) suddenly appear where previously there was absolutely nothing, nothing at all anywhere?

It is at this point that the theist, the believer in God or a god, pounces. The Big Bang was the moment of creation. It was God who caused the Big Bang, and by means of His infinite power brought matter and all its properties and laws into being. Not for nothing, it seems, did the Vatican choose to run a famous conference on the Big Bang in 1981 when the concept was beginning to gather widespread scientific support. At a stroke, both creation and God had become scientifically respectable.

There are, though, at least five difficulties with this conclusion. First, the Big Bang might not actually be the very beginning. It might just mark the point beyond which human investigation cannot go. There might have been something beyond the Big Bang, but that something might be wholly inaccessible to us – in which case, the Big Bang would not be the origin of everything, but only of what we think of as our universe, which actually sprang from something else.

Second (though in opposition to this first thought), the universe might not have had a beginning in time at all. It might be self-contained, like the inside of a sphere. It would be finite, but, as would be said, unbounded. It would have no boundary or edge, spatial or temporal, with space and time both referring only to relationships within the universe. This appears to be the sense of the No Boundary Condition theory of Stephen Hawking, which, according to its protagonist, renders talk of a creator unnecessary.

The idea of a finite but unbounded universe of this sort is clearly difficult to comprehend. A more straightforward way of denying that the universe had a beginning would be simply to assert that it is eternal. It always has existed and always will, so we have no need to speculate about how creation might or might not be possible. (This would, of course, take us back to the first objection.)

Third, even if, against either the eternity or No Boundary Condition views, the universe does have a beginning in time, and there is a moment of creation, it might just have happened without cause or reason. The universe was created by nothing out of nothing.

Theists would say that such a thing is unintelligible, but then their theory of creation also has to postulate an unexplained first cause or event. The difference between theism and atheism is that the theist takes God to be this unexplained thing, whereas the atheist takes it to be the universe itself. The theist gets to God by asking what the cause of the universe is, but apparently feels no similar need to ask what the cause of God is.

In Schopenhauer's image, the theist is like a traveller who dismisses his cab-driver when he gets to his destination. He forgets how it was that he got there and that on arrival he might still need to make a further journey. The point is that no search for causes can ever reach a final resting point without leaving further questions hanging in the air.

The traditional theist will answer this objection by saying that God does not need a cause. God simply exists as the uncaused cause of everything else. God is the being which is self-subsistent, requiring no cause to exist, and on which everything else depends. But the atheist will retort by asking why the universe itself could not be self-subsistent and the uncaused cause of everything which happens within it.

Fourth, how are we supposed to conceive God creating the matter from which the universe is composed? God is supposed to be a spirit, but we have no experience of immaterial spirits bringing matter or material things into existence. More generally, can we envisage any being, even an infinitely powerful one, creating some thing out of nothing? Maybe, as Aristotle thought, matter just is, eternally.

And fifth, even if we concede that the universe does require a divine creator, how do we know that it is anything like the God of religious faith? Does the creator have to be all powerful and all good, as the medievals believed? Aquinas rather optimistically concluded his version of the first-cause argument with the words 'and this is that to which everyone gives the name God'.

But there is a very big jump here. Assuming that something had to bring the universe about, how do we know that it wasn't a slightly malicious or incompetent being, or a being who had no interest in human affairs, or even a committee of eternal intelligences? And even if it is the timeless, all-powerful, all-good, wholly self-sufficient being of medieval Christianity, what has that got to do with the God religious people worship, who is jealous, who is impulsive, who changes His mind in response to our activity, who intervenes in history, who may even in some sense need His creation, and the rest of what is implied in Pascal's God of Abraham, Isaac and Jacob?

So the first-cause argument is not wholly persuasive as a proof of God's existence, though saying this does not mean that claiming that the universe just exists in any way eliminates the mystery of existence.

Also we have, until now, been taking a rather literal interpretation of 'first' in talking of the first cause. We have been assuming that 'first' commits one to a belief in a Big Bang, or some absolutely initial stage of the universe, prior to which there was nothing. We have been assuming that an eternally existing universe would not need a first cause. But in the view of the more sophisticated exponents of the argument, including Aquinas, this assumption is not necessary for it to go through.

Let us assume, in accordance with the first and fourth objections, that matter is eternal. Or, alternatively, in line with the second objection, let us assume that there are no temporal boundaries to the universe. In either case isn't some power still needed to sustain the whole system in existence? What otherwise stops it collapsing into disorder, and ensures that its laws and the properties of matter continue to operate in a regular and predictable way?

In answer to these questions, we are not to think of the first cause as that which would be needed only at the beginning of the universe, if there were a beginning, but rather as something which guides and sustains the universe at every moment. And such a being would be necessary even if the universe had never had a beginning in time.

The relationship between the universe and its first cause would then be rather like that between the sun and life on earth. The sun is a presence whose operation is normally unnoticed; but it is absolutely vital to the maintenance of life, and its absence would cause life to fail. Arguably, seeing God as the ever-present and necessary sustainer of the universe is to take a more religious attitude to existence than if one were to see Him as some remote cause who is needed only at the moment of creation.

This view is still not without difficulties, however. There remains the analogue of our third objection. Who or what sustains God? Nor is it clear how the divine sustaining of the material world is supposed to happen. After all, God is not a material being like the sun, whose effects are certainly physical. And finally, the atheist will say that matter and its operations do not need to be sustained. They do not hang in some sort of state of suspension unless enlivened by a non-material sun. They just are as they are, and that is all that there is to it.

But are they? Can we really accept that systems and laws as complicated as those we find in the universe could just be? Could they have come about through the blind operation of natural forces? In looking at the universe and at our own earth, are we not inevitably led to think of an intelligent designer behind it all?

The argument from design focuses on the degree of orderliness there is in the universe, and it concludes that there could not be that amount of order without the operation of an intelligent designer.

Order is manifested first by the regularity and pre-dictability of all physical processes, ranging in size from immense galaxies to unbelievably tiny particles. Indeed everything in the universe seems to be made up of countless numbers of sub-atomic objects, all of which follow the same patterns of activity, apparently all over the universe. From these basic building-blocks everything else is formed. These bigger things, too, are regular and predictable in their behaviour, in comparatively simple ways, as we have been aware since the time of Newton. But with increasing knowledge of physics, we now realize that the sources of order are far more strange and complex than Newton and his followers envisaged.

The universe, then, is an astonishing combination of simplicity and complexity. Are we not forced to postulate an explanation for degree and extent of its order outside itself? In the view of the theist it cries out for a designer.

Then, when we come to look at life and living processes, over and above the regularity, predictability and complexity of the inorganic realm, we find examples of exquisite functionality. That is to say, in the natural world there are countless examples of organisms whose various parts are precisely adapted to serving the interests of the whole. Thus in the human body, the heart pumps blood, the lungs take in oxygen, the stomach digests food, the eye receives visual stimulation and the brain processes it. Some of these organs, such as the eye, are of an astonishing delicacy and refinement, and very precisely adapted to the circumstances in which they operate. But they are not intelligent in themselves. Surely, it would be said, they must have been designed and given their functions by some intelligent designer.

Similarly, we can wonder at the ways that animals and plants are so closely fitted to the environments in which they live, and at the astonishingly inventive ways in which they exploit the opportunities offered by their surroundings. Yet they themselves do not plan any of this. Isn't this also evidence of planning on the part of an intelligent creator?

Up to the mid-nineteenth century, reasoning of this sort proved immensely powerful and influential in convincing sceptics that even if the Christian religion was not true in all its detail, still the hypothesis of a divine designer was practically unassailable. Only those who were blind to the wonders and intricacies of nature could easily withhold assent. Darwin himself recounts in his autobiography how as a young man the design argument had seemed to him completely convincing.

But, as he tells us, that was before he discovered the law of natural selection. This showed how all the marvellous adaptations and apparent design in nature could be explained by the workings of purely natural and quite unintelligent processes. Nature, unintelligent nature, mimics the activity of a designer. It is enabled to do this because when plants and animals reproduce, some of their offspring manifest differences from their parents and also from others of their kind. They do this for reasons which have nothing to do with any planning for survival, on their part or on the part of anyone else.

Variations are brought about by occasional minute disturbances to their DNA when it is being formed or, in the case of creatures conceived sexually, by the unpredictable way their parents' genes come together. Most of the variations from the existing norm which result prove to be harmful to the creatures who possess them. They and their possessors are killed off in the struggle for survival by a ruthless environment.

Nevertheless, a few of the variations do prove to be beneficial in the battle to survive and reproduce. So the creatures with the advantageous variations survive better and reproduce more. And, as they pass on the advantageous variation to their offspring, the new adaptation becomes embedded in the population, and the basis for further refinements along the same lines. So, it is said, the human eye could have emerged through countless variations working their way through generations of creatures and millions of years from its origins in a primitive light-sensitive cell in one of our remote ancestors.

The precise details of the theory need not concern us.

What is significant is its demonstration of the possibility of spontaneous order, of the emergence of a highly sophisticated system or system of systems without any planning or intelligence. What is needed for the order in nature is not a designer, but just the working out over millions of years of the process of natural selection; that is, through random variations in their make-up of a few members of a given species and the selective retention by the environment of the even fewer successful variations.

In one respect the Darwinian theory of spontaneous order is more realistic than the postulation of a divine designer. There is an awful lot of waste and apparently pointless cruelty in nature. In the processes of evolution there have been an awful lot of false starts and dead ends, and evolution as a whole is fuelled by the inexorable extermination of the unfit, which most species ultimately are.

For all nature's wonders, it is natural to feel that a divine designer blessed with infinite power and wisdom should be able to do better than what we see around us. Any religious view is bound to find suffering and evil a problem, but this is not a difficulty for Darwin who was sensitive to the extent to which nature is far from perfect even in a design sense.

So, can all the order in the universe and not just the natural world be seen as spontaneous? That it can was the view of the Greek and Roman atomists, who were the earliest critics of the design argument. The universe consists of eternal atoms moving around in various configurations. The process is initially random and chaotic, but eventually patterns of stable and regular activity emerge, and, because of the very meaning of stability, tend to be maintained.

Any such account is, of course, highly speculative: but so

is the design argument. Given that neither account can be ruled out as inherently contradictory, the question is whether one is more plausible than the other – or, more generally, is the amount of order there is in the universe such that it would be quite improbable without a divine designer? Given the universe as we experience it, is its order and complexity such that it would be unlikely to have emerged and be maintained without a guiding intelligence?

The questions are good ones, but there is a deep problem in answering them: for any answer we give to them, theistic or atheistic, assumes that we have some sort of way of assessing what might or might not be probable with universes. Is it more probable that a highly ordered universe such as ours needs a designer, or is it more probable that such a universe simply exists or stays in existence on its own? But how do we know what is likely or unlikely in the case of universes?

There is only one universe. We do not have examples of different universes to investigate, with some more ordered, some less ordered, some created, some not. We do not have samples of universes to inspect, to see which ones are closer in nature and constitution to our own, and whether they have creators or not. There is thus no basis for making the relevant judgements. As C. S. Peirce memorably put it, universes are not as plentiful as blackberries: we just have the one. For all the ingenious argument and speculation of theist and atheist alike, its origin and existence remain deeply mysterious.

At this point some religious thinkers will invoke what is called the anthropic principle. Building on what we know of the universe now, and what modern cosmology tells us about its origins at the Big Bang, they will point out that a minuscule difference in the conditions at that moment would have made the world as we know it impossible. More particularly the presence here on earth now of the physical conditions necessary to support conscious life required some very precise and specific conditions in the first few nano-seconds of the universe some 15 billion years ago.

Speculation in this area is known as the anthropic principle because one is starting from the undoubted fact that we (*anthropoi*) exist; and then, with the help of whatever scientific knowledge we have, deducing what must have been true in the very early stages of the universe for our existence, with us in it, to be possible now. It cannot be denied that scientifically this has proved to be a useful approach. It has enabled us to read back into the past what must have been the case for present conditions to exist.

What is less clear, though, is whether anything can be safely concluded from this about any purpose or intention or intelligence which may be behind the whole process. Clearly, whatever conditions were necessary at the start of things to have us, here and now, speculating about the start of things must have been the case. And our existence here and now, as living, thinking, embodied animals, apparently puts some pretty tight and precise constraints on what must have been going on at the Big Bang. But does it follow that those original conditions were put there on purpose to achieve today's state of things? It is hard to see that we are forced to conclude anything of this sort from the anthropic principle. We need to take a step back and look at things in a broader context.

To view the world religiously is to see meaning and

intelligence and purpose behind its mute physical processes. It cannot be said that doing this is wrong, or that science could show that it is wrong. At bottom there can be no conflict between science and religion, provided that each maintains its own proper sphere of influence: that is to say, religion should not, as it has in the past, make claims about the nature of the physical world or about the viability of the theory of evolution. But then equally, science should not insist that its explanations are more complete than they really are, or that there can be nothing but physical reality, as postulated in its theories.

Nor should it attempt to beat down religion by appeals to the size and extent of the universe. That would be a very crude piece of bullying on the part of science. The earth may be small and insignificant astronomically speaking, but that does not imply that there could not be very significant happenings on it from other points of view, or that on it there could not be events of cosmic significance. Maybe, as the anthropic principle implies, we need a universe of the size and extent of ours in order to have consciousness anywhere, even just in one place, even just in this place. And if there were consciousness in just a few places in the universe, or even just in one, would not that place or those places have an eminence which transfigured their physical insignificance?

None of this, though, means that we have to accept the anthropic principle as conclusive proof of an intention behind the universe, or of a purpose going from the Big Bang to human life. There is no way of reading purpose into a sequence of physical events, however complicated, unless they clearly bear the marks of intention and planning.

So, to take the analogy given by William Paley at the start of the nineteenth century, if we found a watch on a deserted heath we would be inclined to think that it had not come into existence by purely natural processes, such as the wind and the rain. We would naturally and reasonably assume that it had been made by a watchmaker and had been dropped by a traveller. But that is because we know how watches and similar devices come about. We are using this knowledge, gained through experience, in order to reason about what is most likely in the case of a watch being on the ground in front of us.

In the case of the processes governing the universe and its development, how such things come about is precisely what is at issue. The universe and most of the things in it are not enough like watches and other human inventions for watchmaking to be a reliable analogy for the construction of the universe.

So, rather than treating the anthropic principle as conclusive proof of the truth of a religious attitude, it would be better to see its espousal as part of what having a religious attitude consists in. It is how someone already attracted to a religious attitude would naturally tend to regard the relevant, rather striking facts; but it is not something forced on us by the facts themselves.

Having said that, however, there is another point which, while in no way affording a proof of any religious view, does argue against a certain type of reductive materialism. We know that life has evolved on earth, and, for all we know, in other parts of the universe as well. For some decades it had been widely assumed that this came about in a fairly simple way, that in certain atmospheric conditions a bolt of lightning hitting the primeval soup would be enough to spark a few molecules into some basic form of bacterial life.

Now unfortunately for this theory, things turn out to be far more complicated. All kinds of components over and above the amino acids originally assumed to constitute the prebiotic broth would have been needed to produce living beings. Indeed, as time and experiments replicating conditions before the start of life have gone on, the broth from which life supposedly emerged has had to be progressively strengthened. Nor was this strengthening just a matter of adding more substances in random fashion. For life to begin, the chemical substances involved need to be in specific, rather particular configurations, chemically speaking. How could this come about without some predisposition on the part of the substances in question to get into the appropriate configurations?

So maybe life did not emerge in simple steps from nonlife. Maybe in the pre-organic world there was already a strong disposition for the chemicals concerned to form themselves into the necessary structures and templates.

If life creates problems for reductive materialism, consciousness presents even greater difficulties. We have a lot of knowledge of the material conditions necessary for consciousness to occur and also of how variations in those conditions are correlated with variations in feeling and perception. But we have no understanding of how the material processes which occur in the brain bring consciousness about. How can material processes give rise to experience? They not only register and react to information, as a robotic machine might do, but they also enable us to feel and sense things and to become self-aware.

What we are talking about here is the difference between a machine and a living, feeling being. This difference may be difficult to characterize, but we all intuitively understand it. On it science is almost wholly unilluminating, as we have seen. It is as if science lacks the concepts even to describe it, let alone to explain it in any substantial sense. Just how can the states of material beings become transparent to themselves? Or is phrasing the question in terms of material beings to set off on the wrong track?

Maybe what we – and science – think of as 'material beings' have properties and dispositions beyond those dealt with in the physical sciences, properties and dispositions foreshadowing life and consciousness. In which case those places in the universe in which there is life and consciousness would not be so insignificant even from a cosmic perspective, despite their small size.

To suggest that life and consciousness might have been pre-figured in the universe from the very start is not in itself to adopt a religious point of view. It is not to say that behind the material face of the universe there is anything like meaning or intelligence. It may just mean that as part of its basic nature the universe has always been disposed to produce meaning and intelligence in beings like us. And maybe saying that is not to go beyond our original deflationary interpretation of the anthropic principle, that whatever is necessary to produce us must have been inherent in nature from the very beginning and contained in its most basic elements.

But when we look at what life and consciousness enable us to do, we can go a little further. Take first our desire to discover truths about the world and our success in doing so.

Now, it could be argued, plausibly enough, that the ability consciously to seek truth and gather truths about our surroundings and our fellows has survival value, and that is why during the course of evolution such an ability was programmed into us.

An evolutionary account of human knowledge will say that the ability to seek and find truths enabled us – or rather our remote ancestors – to anticipate and avoid threats from the environment, and manipulate nature to advantage. It also enabled those who had it to a superior level to outwit other people, and so do better in the reproduction stakes.

But true as all this may be, the evolutionary account does not take us very far when it comes to explaining what we actually know and are interested in. Evolutionary accounts explain organs and faculties in terms of the way they enable their possessors to survive and reproduce. But we have the ability to find out about all sorts of things beyond what would have helped our ancestors to survive on the savannahs of Africa. But this is as far as a strictly evolutionary account could take us, for it is for that that human beings and our faculties evolved, given that biologically speaking there has not been enough time for any significant further evolutionary development within our species.

As examples of non-useful but important knowledge, consider, for example, astrophysics, theorizing about the Big Bang and the resolution of quantum theoretical paradoxes; proofs in the foundations of mathematics and in number theory; knowledge of the history of ancient Greece and of the economy of Cro-Magnon man; speculation about the authorship of the tragedies of Shakespeare and the dating of

Plato's Dialogues; and, finally, philosophy itself. None of these studies contributes directly to survival, nor does the intelligence needed to pursue them have much to do with the evolutionarily produced ability of our ancestors to hunt and gather.

As human beings we have a generalized intelligence and potential for reflection. Whether these things originally emerged in the course of evolution or not, it is clear that we use them in ways which are quite different from anything encompassed within evolutionary theory. We use them to discover the truth about ourselves and about the world for its own sake, and these studies play a significant, non-incidental role in human culture.

Some theorists of evolution claim that the fruits of pure research and of a generalized intelligence can be explained in evolutionary terms. Those who produce such things are widely admired in society, and so receive evolutionary benefits in the form of more desirable mates. But even if it were true that physics laboratories and philosophy departments were magnets for beautiful people, this rather desperate manoeuvre does not really help the evolutionary case.

For it fails to demonstrate why the fruits of pure research into arcane and fundamental questions is admired. It seems that we as humans are – sometimes – driven by a pure desire to know, and to know not just anything but things which have a bearing on the fundamental nature of the world itself and of our human condition. That is why experts in such matters are admired and rewarded, as a by-product of something quite basic in our make-up, and which requires an explanation in its own terms.

If this is so, what then follows about our make-up? According to C. S. Peirce, what follows is that we are not to be

> content with the statement that the searching out of the ideas that govern the universe has no other value than that it helps human animals to swarm and feed. (We should) rather insist that the only thing that makes the human race worth perpetuation is that thereby rational ideas may be developed, and the rationalisation of things furthered.[24]

Peirce's thought is that the universe is an integrated physical-cum-mental system. It has a built-in drive to produce beings who can become conscious of what that system is in both physical and mental aspects. We ourselves are at a pivotal point of this system, being physical and conscious and able to seek out the nature of the system. Through its process of development the universe grows 'knowers', and becomes conscious of itself. However our intelligence originally arose, its scope and nature take us quite beyond standard evolutionary accounts of knowledge. Evolution accounts for it only insofar as it is useful for survival, and this turns out to be a very small aspect of what we are about in our search for knowledge and understanding.

Against this background it becomes plausible to ask where our pure desire to know comes from, and also why our drive to know might be successful even in areas which have nothing to do with survival value. Although our pure desire to know does obviously have some survival value, that is not all it is for. It is not even the most important thing it is for, which may be why it seems attuned even to aspects of reality, knowledge of which has no conceivable bearing on the survival of our primitive hunter-gatherer ancestors, which is roughly where our biological evolution stopped.

Speculation of this sort is indeed speculation. But I contend that it makes more sense of more of our experience than does the reductive materialism which would make life and, above all, consciousness accidental and imponderable by-products of purely physical processes, and which finds considerable difficulty with our drives to know and to philosophize.

Something similar might be said of morality. As with knowledge, it is possible to see part of morality in evolutionary terms. Evolution is about individual survival and reproduction and the competition necessary to sustain individuals, while morality is about co-operation between individuals. But competition and co-operation are not mutually exclusive. Competitors can be helped by co-operating with each other, providing both sides benefit from the co-operation more than if they had simply slugged it out with each other.

As Plato pointed out long ago, even thieves may be better off co-operating in their dishonest enterprises. And if, as modern evolutionary theory would have it, the real force driving biological behaviour is the survival and reproduction of our genes, then I will be motivated to help my children and close relations, for they share my genes to a far greater degree than people to whom I am not related. So evolution can give some account of the way we co-operate with our kin and our children, and of the way we are all ready to co-operate with non-kin on a tit-for-tat basis.

But this is very far from being a complete account of

morality. Morality is not just about helping our relations or those who can help us, and even where it is, the motive is not supposed to be self-interest. All moral codes say that in acting morally we should be showing concern for the needs and rights of others. Morality is essentially other-regarding. In being moral we are to do our duty to others and show compassion to others for the sake of their well-being.

It may be that a system in which people do look to the interests of others is, overall, of mutual benefit. But unless I really care for the interests of others, that does not give me a reason to enter into the system. I could simply be pleased that such a system existed, and profit from its existence, from outside, as it were, insofar as the system benefited me.

But free-riding of this sort is excluded by morality; in a moral system we are each supposed to respect the basic rights of others, regardless of benefit to ourselves. Even if there is no conceivable way in which the other might be able to compensate us for what we do for him or her, we are to do our duty by him or her. We are supposed to accord the other respect simply by virtue of his or her humanity, the very existence of which imposes a demand on us.

This unconditional respect for other human beings is part of the meaning of the piety referred to in Chapter 5. Now it is true that piety of this sort cannot be justified in terms of self-interest. By its very nature it operates beyond the bounds of self-interest. If rationality is conceived in terms of what would benefit me, then piety and indeed morality are irrational.

They are certainly irrational so long as we remain within the confines of what helps me or my genes to survive and reproduce. They will on occasion demand that I do things which run counter to my own survival and reproduction, as we saw in the case of Socrates. 'Let justice be done, though the heavens fall', said the Roman poet, but similar sentiments abound in Christianity, Buddhism, Islam and many other religious and ethical systems.

On the other hand, if being rational is understood to encompass other-regarding virtues and reasons for actions which benefit others as well as the agent, then there is nothing irrational about piety or morality. As a matter of fact and experience, we all do admit the cogency of reasons of this sort, even though we are not always swayed by them when it comes to acting. But how is it that we are made so as to feel the force of truly other-regarding reasons? How is it that, like Socrates, we seem naturally disposed to go beyond the narrow version of rationality afforded by evolutionary considerations?

A natural thought at this point would be to see us as part of a wider system of feeling and consciousness. Just as we can get to know how things are in the universe, by being part of a drive within the universe towards thought and understanding, so are we to see ourselves as part of a whole greater than our individual selves, in which we owe obligations of respect and compassion to other beings within that whole. These obligations to others will be the greater the more conscious and rationally developed the beings in question.

Insofar as we are part of this wider whole and our nature and identity constituted by being part of it, we do ourselves damage by seeking our own individual survival at the expense of our obligations to the wider whole. No doubt from the Socratic point of view, these wider obligations will include the cultivation of intellectual virtues such as truthfulness and integrity – which further the rationalization of things – as well as the obviously moral duties of compassion and respect for other persons, which would follow directly from our being part of a wider world of consciousness, striving and suffering.

But, as again we know from experience, the world of living, conscious beings is not simply one of suffering. It is also a world of beauty and aesthetic consolation. It is a world in which we as conscious physical beings can feel ourselves at home through finding aesthetic delight in what surrounds us.

Through aesthetic experience we also gain a sense of penetrating to the essence of things. In aesthetic experience we experience the everyday world not as a thing to be used, but as a locus of value for its own sake. In this mood the world is not something to be understood on a merely theoretical level, but, endowed with beauty, it becomes the subject of our admiration and love. At times, in aesthetic reverie – in experiencing what the eighteenth-century theorists called the sublime – we sense a power and a transcendence which is quite beyond what is given to us in the manipulations and administrations with which everyday life is largely filled.

None of this will amount to a proof of any religion or even of anything religious. These reflections on knowledge, morality and aesthetics are not offered as a proof of the existence of God. But they are offered as an indication of the way in which certain key aspects of our life and experience may be seen as pointing in a religious or quasi-religious direction.

As we see from the inconclusiveness of the traditional

arguments for the existence of God, the physical world is religiously ambivalent. But we may still be able to see the religious impulse to understand the world in more than physical terms as emerging from within our experience.

The religious impulse might be seen as stemming from our urge to understand the world as it is in itself; then from our sense that we have certain absolute duties, which we have neither chosen nor can abrogate; and finally from our experience of a natural object or work of art as beautiful, which suggests that the perfection we long for in some other world may on occasion actually be realized in this.

A sense of the unconditional nature of these feelings will undoubtedly be sustained by a mature religious faith. For many religious people, at least, it will make sense only on the assumption that the universe is not a purely physical thing, and that it is either guided by a personal force which these feelings reveal or that it has in itself properties other than the straightforwardly physical or possibly even both.

Certainly purely secular accounts of morality and aesthetics and of our search for knowledge, such as those offered by evolutionary theorists, will have difficulty accounting for the absoluteness of moral obligation, for the apparently timeless sense of rightness and transcendence of some aesthetic experiences, and even of our drive to pure research and its success. Creatures subject to the constraints of evolutionary theory should not be so successful in acquiring knowledge of realities so far removed from what we have evolved to cope with. Nor should they continue to feel the absoluteness of moral obligation or the transcendence of the aesthetic once they realize their true nature and origins.

Reductive accounts of human nature are indeed

prevalent. Science and morality are seen as survival devices, the latter filled out with the mathematics of game theory. Aesthetics is analysed in terms of satisfactions produced by brain chemistry. But, as I have attempted to show, these accounts falsify the experience in each case. But, perhaps even more striking and even more problematic for the reductivist, the accounts seem so far to have no tendency to impede the activities in question, or our understanding of them in their unreduced forms. That is to say, even as we develop accounts which would undermine their motivation and possibility, we continue to interpret key aspects of our form of life at their face value. We continue to think that the pursuit of knowledge for its own sake is both desirable and possible. We continue to think of moral demands as absolute, and to admire those who act on them in that way. And we continue to regard the experience of beauty as both significant and revelatory.

All this argues against reductionism about human life. At the very least, it leaves room for an understanding of our condition, which if not itself religious, explains why over millennia people have been drawn to religion. For the roots of religion lie within our experience of the world and of our humanity.

9 **Death**

At the end of the last chapter we indicated that there are key aspects of human life and experience which cannot be seen in purely materialistic terms. Our search for knowledge, our moral sense and the appreciation of beauty all extend our horizons beyond those of survival and reproduction. The phenomenon of consciousness is hard even to describe in terms drawn from the physical sciences. So central is consciousness to our life that it is impossible to see it as a mere by-product of physical forces and events.

There is, then, a sense that through our conscious experience and particularly through the activities mentioned we do touch on aspects of the very fabric of the universe which are not revealed in the physical sciences. Should this give us hope?

As human beings we are conscious not just of things around us. We are conscious of our existence as physical beings and we are also conscious that this existence is temporally finite. We know that there was a time when we did not exist. We also know that there will be a time when we will no longer exist.

We know that we will die. We know that our own personal stream of consciousness which throws light on reality will be turned off. We know that as far as each of us is concerned, the darkness before we existed will return. With death, one unique perspective on the world will be extinguished for ever: ours, and that will be the end of it.

In this acute sense of our own mortality we are distinct from animals. Animals, we may suppose, are conscious of the present moment. But they lack language and the ability to conceptualize beyond the immediate present. They lack any sense of fate or of their own inevitable individual fate.

For the existentialists there is an intimate connection between awareness of our mortality and self-consciousness. Self-consciousness involves a sense of one's uniqueness. In being conscious of oneself, one is aware of this one unique journey through the world, and how it is different from every other. It is the realization that the journey will end which brings its uniqueness home most acutely. One is not simply the same as all the rest. By reflecting on one's own death, one understands that though one is part of a group, one is also unique.

Perhaps if one thought about the time before one's birth, the realization would be the same. But there is a vital difference between a light gradually coming up, as we grow from infancy to self-consciousness, and, its once being fully up, then being suddenly turned off.

We did not suffer before we were alive. Before we were alive we were aware of nothing. Most of us do not feel a sense of loss that we did not experience the world prior to our birth. For most of us, this is not a source of regret or of fear.

We will not suffer once we are dead. After we are dead we will be aware of nothing. But, unlike the time before we were born, most of us do feel regret that we will not still be alive after the time of our death. We fear our future non-existence in contrast to our indifference about our past non-existence.

Why this asymmetry between our attitude to the time before our birth and that after our death? It must have something to do with our different relationship to past and future, and in particular with the way our plans and projects look to the future. We cannot affect the past, but we can affect the future.

The past is like the soil from which we spring into consciousness. We are initially formed by it, and have no effect on it. But once we have emerged into the light, we start to affect things. We make our mark on the world by the way we affect the present and the future.

When we die, so much that we have started will be left incomplete. Experiences we may have envisaged having will not be had. Apart from the pain and suffering involved in dying, dying is like being shut out of a party one wanted to be invited to. By contrast, before one's birth there was no one to anticipate being excluded.

Some people terminate their existence before their natural death. This is, in a way, doubly regrettable. Such people are unable to see enough virtue in what is actually before them or in the likely course of their future. For them life is not worth living. But this does not mean that they leave the world without intense sadness that it was not different from how it actually was. They also regret the future there might have been had things been different.

For some, the very fact that life is finite casts a shadow over the present. The light will be snuffed out, as if they never were – or so they reason. Does this mean that their efforts now are worthless? For what they do now is of no significance after their death.

One can, of course, dispute that on a literal level. My efforts will have significance after my death, through my deeds and my children. But the significance surely decreases as time goes on. For most of us, in a few generations it will indeed be as if we have never lived.

So, does death make our efforts while alive worthless or absurd? Is there any point in the pain and inevitable suffering of life if all comes to naught? The regret involved in leaving life and the very fact of death casts a pall over life itself. Bold talk of making a stain on the silence is so much whistling in the dark, for in the end there is only silence, only dark.

There are various responses to this sort of pessimism. Some, in a sense, embrace it, finding advantage in their mortality. All life is suffering, so it is good that it ends. And even if all life is not suffering, a lot of it is. Living for ever would be unutterably tedious, at best. The risk and urgency which comes from the finiteness of our lives and the ever-present danger of death gives our projects an edge and a meaning they would otherwise lack.

But these responses hardly solve the main enigma. If life is suffering or tedious, what is the point of living at all? Would it not have been better not to live at all, as the ancient Greek wisdom had it: and if one has to live, then better to die soon? And does not the inevitable transience of our projects, which is brought about by death, undermine our reason for engaging in them?

So perhaps we should look just to the quality of each experience as and when we have it, and forget about the future or our ending. As Walter Pater put it,

> not the fruit of experience, but experience itself, is the end. A counted number of pulses only is given to us of a variegated, dramatic life. How may we see in them all that is to be seen in them by the finest senses? How shall we pass most swiftly from point to point, and be present always at the focus where the greatest number of vital forces unite in their purest energy? To burn always with this hard, gem-like flame, to maintain this ecstacy, is success in life.[25]

And he goes on to say that to fall victim to habit, and to fail to 'discriminate every moment some passionate attitude in those about us' is 'on this short day of frost and sun, to sleep before evening'.

The trouble here is that we are given no reason to look to anything other than the present moment. It cuts us off from the past and the future and ultimately from our fellows. It also seems to require a constant quest for ever more exotic and extreme experience, a quest surely doomed to failure, as every gourmet and every Don Giovanni knows only too well.

There is something solipsistic about it, if not plain selfish. Given that some of our most enduring satisfactions are those which involve the well-being of others, there may be something self-defeating about it too.

Nevertheless the fact of death and connected aspects of our mortality put certain types of earthly hope in perspective. These come in two main forms. There is first the political promise, that through some radical change in our social arrangements it will be possible to build a utopia, a heaven on earth. Then, second, there is the scientific dream, that through medical advances, particularly those in genetics, it will be possible to rid mankind of its traditional sources of unhappiness and allow us all to live far longer and far healthier than had ever been thought possible.

The real point is not that we should not strive for better political arrangements, better health and longer lives. The real point is that even when such things have been achieved, we will still be prey to our most pressing dilemmas. However long we live, we will eventually die. Whatever our political arrangements or physical and intellectual prowess, we will still be subject to the vagaries of fate. None of us can avoid, sooner or later, the heartache of personal rejection and lack of fulfilment. And we will still be subject in our own individual lives and behaviour to the innate selfishness and viciousness which lurks within us all, and which religious writers attribute to original sin.

In view of all this, it is pure fantasy to believe that a utopia might be possible. Neither politics nor science can alter the fundamental facts of our nature and our limitations. To the extent that political and scientific utopias simply fail to come to terms with the unpleasant realities of the human condition, this is not a purely neutral point.

Because their projected solutions take no account of the unalterable facts of our nature and destiny, they make these facts that much harder to confront and to deal with. People should not be unhappy in an earthly paradise. If they are, it shows that they are sick or deluded. They need treatment or re-education.

But, as twentieth-century history has amply demonstrated, that response paves the way to hell. Politically it paves the way to the gulag as a punishment for dissent. And in the affluent West it leads to the therapeutic society in which common-or-garden angst is treated as a form of impermissible madness, and in which people are offered pills for their heartache.

Heartache and a sense of our limitation and mortality are not signs of madness, and cannot be eased by therapy. Nor is it heresy to point to the irrelevance of politics to our most basic problems and to the way that the most idealistic and egalitarian of political projects have a curious habit of rewarding those driving them and of impoverishing the rest. On the contrary, a lively awareness of all these points is necessary for a more constructive and positive attitude to human life.

Awareness of death and a sense of our limitations, personal and social, are necessary for any sort of genuine progress, personal or social. This is not to say that death and our limitations suddenly become good or less than tragic. To see them as good would be to minimize them and to demean the suffering of those afflicted and grieving.

Nor is any lasting solution to be found in the narrow aestheticism of a Walter Pater. That, too, is an ultimately unavailing attempt to deny the seriousness of our problems and the chilling finality of death. It is also an avoidance of the ultimately unsatisfying nature of hedonism. For there is something mechanistic and dispiriting about a life lived in pursuit of pleasures, whether they be refined or gross. And given the insatiability of appetite, such a life is doomed to unhappiness and the psychiatrist's couch.

What we need to cultivate is the sense that our own pleasures and even our own individual fates are not ends in themselves. We need to build on those intimations of wider perspectives which we explored in the last chapter.

We can see ourselves as part of an unfolding of awareness

in the universe as a whole, and in which our pursuit of knowledge and understanding are part of a co-operative quest for an emerging harmony between us and nature. We might also see this process, as Peirce did, as part of nature's own unfolding. We as conscious seekers after truth play a central role in nature's self-development and increasing self-awareness. Or, from an orthodox theistic point of view, our understanding of the world would be a matter of gaining insight into the mind of the creator.

Then we can see our moral sense as promoting a realization that there are values which transcend our individual fate and which may be more important than our own life. These values include such virtues as respect for others and for our surroundings. In our own life they will include personal integrity and faithfulness to our commitments, combined with a sense that we diminish ourselves if we let ourselves down here, however long we live or how well rewarded we are. In both public and private spheres we will value justice, truthfulness, loyalty and courage.

All these virtues may, at the extreme, be more important than life itself, as Socrates argued in his prison. Through their practice, we come to see ourselves as individuals as bound to other individuals, living, dead and as yet unborn. We may also begin to cultivate an attitude of piety to our society and to the world itself. We will see ourselves as joined with others in the construction of a moral fabric at least as real and as important as the world of physical fact.

We can cultivate aesthetic experience not as momentary pleasure disconnected from the rest of life, but as a source of theoria. In it we would find conscious realization of an underlying harmony within the universe and also between us and the universe. Here particularly the presence of evil and suffering, the unbearable pettiness of much of our existence and once again the fact of death, might seem to threaten. The hope would be that theoria might indicate that these things are not the whole story, that despite these things, and in our confronting of these things, there is something of enduring value. And perhaps that in rising above the negative aspects of existence we help to create that value.

What is being suggested here is not that death is not terrible: death is terrible for each one of us, and terrible too when we see the deaths of those we love and know. Nevertheless there are intimations of value within our experience which reveal us each to be part of something more significant than our individual life and fate. Seeing our life in this way may help to take away some of the sting of death.

In the past these intimations of value have typically been expressed and understood religiously. They have underpinned the doctrines and works of religions. Morality, art and science itself have been brought under the aegis of religion. Within the West, at least, they flourished under the protection of religion for centuries, even though in the end science proved instrumental in undermining religion.

With the growth of science and with the advance of materialism, formal religion has declined. But the intimations of value survive, and they are resistant to being explained away in materialistic fashion. That is to say, attempts to explain our search for knowledge and our moral and aesthetic senses systematically distort what we experience in each case. Consciousness itself is difficult to see within a materialistic perspective.

Whether these reflections should lead us to consider or reconsider any actual religion is not for philosophy to say. Philosophy, working within what can be ascertained by reason alone, can at most clear a space for more full-bloodied world-views and commitments. It is, though, obvious that some religions would seek at this point to develop a doctrine of the survival of death. That is to say, they would take our intimations of a higher value as an indication that we are destined for some non-bodily form of existence after death, just as Socrates did.

There are serious problems with the notion of survival of death. How, for example, are experience or thought possible without a body? How, in the absence of limbs and organs, could we be said to act? How, without any physical way of connecting our ideas and intentions to the world or to others, could we change things in the world or communicate? At the very least, it looks as if any post-mortem existence is going to be very different from our present life, rooted as it is in our bodily nature.

On the other hand, if survival simply means that we are subsumed into some greater reality, what becomes of the individual person that I am now, and whose death is a matter of such concern to me?

Despite these difficulties, religious faith may furnish a hope that some form of personal survival is possible, or that some form of impersonal survival could be meaningful. It cannot be said that the difficulties rule out either possibility completely. But, given their seriousness, survival of death remains a case where philosophy would need considerable supplementation for belief to be credible.

At the same time, as I hope to have shown, philosophy

can help us to understand that our everyday experience contains insights and values which enable us to see ourselves – and our deaths – as part of processes larger than our individual lives. Against this background, while death is individually tragic, it would be wrong to see it as the extermination of all our hopes. On the contrary, faithfulness to our hopes may, in the extreme case, as with Socrates, require the choice of an honourable death over a dishonourable life. In such circumstances, what would be truly tragic, and the ending of all most of us care about, would be the choice of life over death.

10 Philosophy and the Promise

According to Aristotle, the highest activity of which human beings are capable is philosophical contemplation. In this we fulfil our nature as rational beings. Reason is our highest and most distinctive capacity, and in philosophy we engage in reasoning in its purest form. We contemplate the truths of eternity and the divine intelligence which directs all things, and to which all things ultimately tend.

Of course, Aristotle believed, not all human beings are capable of this form of contemplation. Some men are by nature slaves; the intellectual capacity of women is inferior to that of men. For those who could not think for themselves, the best they can do is to find masters who would do their thinking for them, although they do have the intelligence to see the need for that.

I imagine that most people in the contemporary world would be repelled by much of this. They would be repelled by its élitism. They would be repelled by the thought that many people are better off having others to do their thinking and take their decisions for them. They would be repelled by what would be described as Aristotle's sexism.

Aristotle is surely wrong to dismiss the intellectual capacity of women in the way he does, but there may still be something in what he says about the overall distribution of intellectual powers. At least, as an empirical fact there has been no society in the history of the world in which the majority of the population has engaged in philosophical reflection of the type Aristotle was interested in, or even of the type exemplified in this book.

'Philosophy for all' may be a commendable and pious aspiration, but at least for the foreseeable future it is bound to remain an aspiration. People are interested in many different things. Even after a century or more of compulsory education, comparatively few are interested in things of the mind. This may go some way to explaining why intellectuals, including philosophers, frequently disparage the ambitions and interests of ordinary people.

This is not an edifying characteristic. Insofar as they exhibit it, intellectuals, including philosophers, deserve the disdain in which they themselves are held by large numbers of their contemporaries, who, insofar as they think about these matters at all, feel justified in their neglect of things of the mind.

Actually Aristotle, for all his straightforward élitism, did not disparage the tastes and ambitions of ordinary people. His view, at least as exemplified in his practice, was that while only a few would actually think philosophically, in their thinking they would actually vindicate the morality and tastes of ordinary, decent people.

In this, he was quite different from Plato, whose ambition was to set up an entirely new type of society on purely philosophical principles. In similar vein, as we have seen, the upshot of much contemporary philosophy is to suggest that there is something radically wrong with the commonsense belief that the world is replete with such things as colour, sound, taste, texture and smell.

Much contemporary philosophy also suggests a revisionary attitude to many of our basic moral and political loyalties and beliefs. This is true both of straightforward Anglo-Saxon utilitarianism, and also, more radically, of philosophy inspired by the European fashion for unmasking and deconstructing our moral and political fabric, by showing it to be a device for dominating and repressing the masses.

The spirit of this book is, in a significant sense, Aristotelian. That is to say, its aim has been to get a degree of perspective on what we do, and for a time to take us out of what Newman called the flow of life. But in gaining perspective and distance by reflecting on things normally taken for granted, we have tended to vindicate ordinary human reality, not to undermine it.

We have tried to show that in our basic orientation to the world we emerge as embodied agents who perceive things as they are. We are also free persons, motivated by ideals such as truth, goodness and beauty. Some of what we do, and some of what we inherit through our culture and upbringing, goes some way to realizing these ideals.

Despite the arguments of scientific materialists, it makes nonsense of our experience and activity to see ourselves and those we live with as merely unwitting victims of biological or physical forces. Our freedom and our reason allow us to transcend our physical origins, and make something of our lives for ourselves.

No more are we inevitably imprisoned in social structures against our will and against our reason, as the proponents of deconstruction would have it. Sometimes we do see ourselves or others as systematically deceived and manipulated, but this condition is neither universal nor inescapable. Through reason, thought and discussion, through philosophy, we can each ascend to a higher viewpoint.

Moreover, even without explicit philosophical reflection, people eventually see through propaganda and indoctrination which is purely that, and which has no basis in any sort of reality. As became clear in the later days of the communist empire, even ordinary people have an inherent tendency to discriminate truth from lies, even lies of the most pervasive and systematic sort.

And in most of what most of us do most of the time, against the background into which we are born, to be sure, we make our own choices and exercise responsibility for what we do and believe. To suppose otherwise is to make a mockery of how we regard ourselves and others. This is just as true of how we regard the doings of those remote from our own mentality as it is with those with whom we share a common culture.

Part of what it means to see another as a human being is to see him or her as able to act for the best, and in the light of what appears as true and beautiful. And if for some others what counts as truth, goodness and beauty are very different from what they are for us, the fact that we each aspire to truth, goodness and beauty as they are in themselves, and not just as they seem to one group, provides the basis for a liberating discussion.

It is true that a philosophical perspective is not attained by most people for any length of time, and not by anyone all the time. It is also true that in our philosophical reflections, at least, we have not undermined ordinary human reality. We have defended much of the ordinary perspective against potential assault from a number of quarters.

But we have not simply remained at the level of unreflective common sense. There has been a movement in our thinking from unreflective immersion in the flow of life to thought about what is implicit in our commonsensical beliefs and activities, and about what we all in practice live by, whatever our theoretical stance. We have endeavoured to show that at the heart of our life and activity there are pointers to aspects of reality which are not narrowly materialistic, and which are not captured by science.

Insofar as public discourse tends to ignore any such possibility, philosophy can take us beyond the everyday. Something of the Aristotelian promise is thus redeemed. We move towards theoria, towards a non-religious form of contemplation. Things which we all, in a sense know, but know darkly, can be brought into the open in philosophical reflection.

So, in everyday life, we value the search for knowledge for its own sake, and we are committed to virtues like truth-seeking and logical consistency. In philosophy we can ask ourselves what is presupposed by such capacities. We can think about the inadequacy of accounting for such things in biological or evolutionary terms; thus logic and hence thought itself rely on a sense of correctness which is absolute, and our desire to know far transcends what there is any use in knowing.

We can take the phenomenon of consciousness and bring home to ourselves its mysteriousness from a physical point of view. Together, consciousness and our attitudes to logic and knowledge suggest that seeing ourselves as biological survival machines is woefully inadequate.

Similarly the moral sense which permeates our lives, and on which any civilized form of existence depends, requires that we all accept that there are values with an authority over us which holds come what may. It is hard to account for this sense in terms of a social contract or of what might be conducive to one's self-interest. Equally purely evolutionary explanations can only give us duties and obligations where there is some profit for the individual in recognizing them. Faced with this difficulty for evolutionary theory, some philosophers, of whom Nietzsche was a forerunner, profess to find morality itself incoherent or outdated. Others would see morality in terms of the struggle of one class or group against another.

But are they able to live their own lives without moral beliefs and attitudes, without in their own behaviour striving to discover what is really for the best, irrespective of evolutionary gain or class advantage? Another, more robust, reaction would be that of Socrates: that morality, being so fundamental an aspect of our lives, suggests the limitations of naturalistic accounts of human existence and the superficiality of the view that moral and other values simply serve the interests of the stronger.

And so does our aesthetic interest, in the way it implies a more than physical harmony within existence in general, and between our experience and our world in particular. We need to stress that aesthetic satisfaction is more than a physical pleasure. There is something irreducibly cognitive about it, even in music and in abstract art, where there may be no information transmitted. But there should nevertheless be a sense conveyed of the rightness of what is perceived, emotionally, intellectually, spiritually even. The intellect and the feelings as well as the senses will be engaged. But it will be the intellect and feelings as working in and through the senses, and not, as in science, intellect apart from senses and feeling, or, as at times in morality, against them. In aesthetic experience all aspects of our existence are bound together – spiritual, physical, emotional, intellectual, concrete and abstract, joyful and sad, comic and tragic. It is this harmonizing of all of what we are which lies behind Nietzsche's early aphorism, that it is only as an aesthetic phenomenon that existence and the world are eternally justified.[26]

Philosophy in its explicit sense may not be for everyone. But it may be good for everyone that it is done. At least it may be good for everyone if its impact is not to curb the ambition of the spirit.

What I hope I might have shown that philosophy can do is to awaken our sensitivity to realities which underpin our ordinary lives and activities, and which show that in our ordinary, everyday lives there are extraordinary aspects. At least, from a purely naturalistic point of view they may be extraordinary. These are things which are usually just out of sight of unreflective consciousness, but they are things which we all know, but darkly.

Philosophy is not religion, neither is it wisdom in any substantive sense. But at our current stage of history and culture, with religion in decline and crass materialism and philistinism in the ascendant, philosophy can have a vital role in recovering the full meaning of our humanity. It can pave the way for wisdom, even if it does not directly supply it. At the start of the twenty-first century, that is both philosophy's promise and the challenge it is set.

Notes and References

1. Nicholas Capaldi, *The Enlightenment Project in the Analytic Conversation*, Kluwer Academic Publishers, Dordrecht, 1998, p. 454.
2. Martin Heidegger, 'Beiträge zur Philosophie (Vom Ereignis)', Section 259, *Gesamtausgabe*, Vol. 65 (1989), p. 435.
3. Martin Heidegger, 'Address to German Students', 3 November 1933; discussed and quoted in Herman Philipse's *Heidegger's Philosophy of Being*, Princeton University Press, 1998, p. 251.
4. Martin Heidegger, 'Lecture on Schelling', 1936, Section 3a, *Gesamtausgabe*, Vol. 42, pp. 40–1. This passage, its omission from later versions of the lecture and its eventual restoration in the collected works are all discussed by Philipse, *op. cit.*, pp. 250–1 and 498.
5. Plato, *Phaedo*, quoted here as in the translation by Hugh Tredennick in *The Last Days of Socrates*, Penguin Books, Harmondsworth, 1969. *Phaedo* is dated to around 368 BC, more than two decades after Socrates' death in 399 BC.
6. Alan Sokal and Jean Bricmont, *Intellectual Imposures*, Profile Books, London, 1998; contains the original paper from *Social Text* and extensive discussion of it.
7. Stephen Hawking, *A Brief History of Time*, Bantam Press, London, 1988, p 175.
8. René Descartes, *Meditations* (1641), especially Meditations 1 and 2.
9. As described in the *Republic*.
10. See the edition of *Utilitarianism* by John Stuart Mill (1861), edited by Mary Warnock (which includes extracts from Bentham and other works by Mill), Fontana, London, 1962, pp. 123 and 260.

11. Edmund Burke, *Reflections on the Revolution in France* (1790), Penguin Books, Harmondsworth, 1986, pp. 194–5.
12. John Rawls, *A Theory of Justice*, Oxford University Press, 1972.
13. Burke, *op. cit.*, p. 171.
14. Edward O. Wilson, *Biophilia*, Harvard University Press, 1984.
15. cf. Roger Scruton, *Animal Rights and Wrongs* (Third Edition), Metro Books, London, 2000, pp. 64–8.
16. Marcel Proust, *Rememberance of Things Past*, Vol. XI, translated by C. K. Scott Moncrieff, Chatto and Windus, London, 1969, p. 320.
17. John Ruskin, *Modern Painters* (1856), Vol. 3, Part 4, penultimate paragraph; in the Library Edition of Ruskin's works, edited by E. T. Cook and Alexander Wedderburn, George Allen, London, 1903–12, Vol. 5, p. 387.
18. Rainer Maria Rilke, *Duino Elegies*, translated by J. B. Leishman and Stephen Spender, Chatto and Windus, London, 1975, p. 25.
19. Immanuel Kant, *Critique of Judgement* (1790).
20. David Hume, *Of the Standard of Taste* (1757), paragraph 11.
21. Ruskin, *Modern Painters*, Vol. 5, Part 9, *loc. cit.*, pp. 294–5.
22. Arthur C. Danto, *Philosophizing Art*, University of California Press, Berkeley and Los Angeles, 1999, pp. 134–5.
23. On this aspect of Ruskin's thought, cf. Peter Fuller, *Theoria*, Chatto and Windus, London, 1988, especially Chapter 4, from which the quotations are taken.
24. C. S. Peirce, 'Review of Clark University, 1889–99', in *Science*, 1900, pp. 620–2; quoted in Charles S. Peirce, *Selected Writings*, edited by P. Wiener, Dover Publications, New York, 1958, pp. 333–4.
25. Walter Pater, *The Renaissance: Studies and Art and Poetry* (1873), edited by Kenneth Clark, Fontana, London, 1961, pp. 222–3.
26. This is the core thesis of Nietzsche's first work *The Birth of Tragedy* (1871). It should be noted that even in that work, Nietzsche himself saw redemption arising from the illusions of art. Even then it was unclear how far for Nietzsche artistic illusion revealed reality.

Name Index